Indexing Specialties: Web Sites

By Heather Hedden

AMERICAN SOCIETY OF INDEXERS

First Printing, 2007

Indexing Specialties: Web Sites

ISBN 978-1-57387-302-4

Copyright © 2007 by American Society of Indexers, Inc.

All rights reserved. No part of this book may be reproduced in any form by any electronic or mechanical means, including information storage and retrieval systems, without the express written permission from the Society except by a reviewer who may quote brief passages for a review.

Publisher's Note: The editor and publisher have taken care in preparation of this book but make no expressed or implied warranty of any kind and assume no responsibility for errors or omissions. No liability is assumed for incidental or consequential damages in connection with or arising out of the use of the information or programs contained herein.

Many of the designations used by manufacturers and sellers to distinguish their products are claimed as trademarks. Where those designations appear in this book and Information Today, Inc. was aware of a trademark claim, the designations have been printed with initial capital letters.

Published by
Information Today, Inc.
143 Old Marlton Pike
Medford, NJ 08055

in association with

The American Society of Indexers, Inc.
10200 West 44th Avenue
Suite 304
Wheat Ridge, CO 80033

Printed in the United States of America

President and CEO: Thomas H. Hogan, Sr.
Editor-in-Chief and Publisher: John B. Bryans
Managing Editor: Amy Reeve
VP Graphics and Production: M. Heide Dengler
Book Designer: Kara Mia Jalkowski
Copy Editor: Dorothy Pike
Proofreader: Kathleen Spaltro
Indexer: Linda Kenny Sloan

Contents

Foreword, by Seth Maislin v

Introduction vii

    Chapter 1:   Introduction to Web Site Indexes 1

    Chapter 2:   HTML Basics 13

    Chapter 3:   HTML for Indexes 29

    Chapter 4:   Book Indexing Software for Creating Web Indexes 43

    Chapter 5:   XRefHT for Creating Web Indexes 61

    Chapter 6:   HTML Indexer for Creating Web Indexes 79

    Chapter 7:   Web Site Indexing Techniques 99

    Chapter 8:   Web Site Index Style and Format 117

    Chapter 9:   Web Index Market and Business 135

About the Author 155

Index, by Linda Kenny Sloan 157

Foreword

Indexing is not a popular profession by any stretch of the imagination. Not only is it almost completely unknown in lay circles, but let's be honest: Writing indexes sounds about as exciting as cleaning the house, but a hundred times harder. Also, if you were born in any year before 1990, the idea of "Web site indexing" sounds like cleaning a house in outer space. I mean, there *are* no houses in outer space.

The Internet and the Web—this monstrously huge and growing system of sharing data—desperately need more information sorcerers like Heather Hedden. Not only does Heather have the talent to recognize when knowledge is missing, but she also has the ability to make that knowledge visible. She starts by learning for herself, and then she loves to share.

Heather and I first crossed paths in my classroom, where I taught a course called "Writing Indexes for Books and Websites." My course was written to explore the questions and theories of indexing and so couldn't be limited to just books. Heather's interest went much further, and since then she has explored writing Web indexes as a singular discipline. For me, Heather has been a student, an apprentice, and a role model. She's someone I count on to get things done. She has vaulted across the lines from library science to book indexing to Web indexing, each time with surprising success, and has since become a renowned and respected expert in the Web indexing community.

Indexing Specialties: Web Sites is a book filled with honest, get-it-done advice. Heather is not afraid to talk about the code and the tools because she has faith in her readers. In her hands, the complicated stuff *looks* straightforward. Besides, when the technical lessons are over, Heather shows readers how to *think* about Web indexing as well—as a process and as a business. Until now, if book indexers wanted to graduate to the Internet frontier, they had no unified place of reference, no single source of everything they'd want to know. In fact, some of the tools Heather includes in this book were almost completely unknown to indexers until now.

I am excited and pleased to see Heather compiling this knowledge in a book. She has put into print an indexer's Rosetta Stone, which will lead book indexers toward other information management topics like taxonomies, information architecture, and search tools. It's not about complicated coding practices and computer programs, but about the guidelines to getting that A-to-Z index published on the Internet and about doing it right.

She begins by exploring the boundaries of Web site indexing, clarifying what kinds of sites need indexing, how they should look, and how they should work. Then she immediately provides the HTML building blocks to making your indexes appear on the Web, the surprisingly simple code you need to create index pages, index entries, indentations, hyperlinks, and cross-reference links. If you've never programmed on the Web before and are afraid it's over your head, you'll be kicking yourself once you see how easy Heather makes it.

Once you're armed with the grammar, you next need the tools to actually write. Heather gives you the detail about the tools (CINDEX, HTML Indexer, HTML/Prep, Macrex, SKY Index Professional, and XRefHT) to create or generate indexes that are ready for Web publication. She takes the most time exploring the specialized tools of XRefHT and HTML Indexer, two stand-alone Web indexing applications, and shows how you can use their features with agility.

The last third of the book is dedicated to the "mindspace" of Web indexing. There's more to indexing than just the tools, and so Heather writes carefully about how indexers should approach the job. She addresses the challenges of working out of order, adding anchors, indexing periodicals, and knowing which pages and at what level of detail you should index. She deals in detail with cross-references, language, subentry structure, and format. Finally, Heather dives into the nitty-gritty of the Web indexing marketplace, including how to market yourself as a Web site indexer.

Indexing Specialties: Web Sites is going to satisfy you immediately and in the long term. On behalf of the American Society of Indexers—and myself, personally—I am honored to welcome Heather as an esteemed author in our community.

—Seth Maislin
President of the American Society of Indexers (2006–2007)

Introduction

The idea to write this book came from a workshop I have given online and at indexing conferences. More and more, indexers are being asked to adapt their print indexes to the electronic environment or to write indexes specifically for Web sites. From the enthusiastic reception of the workshop attendees, I could see a need to write a book that provides step-by-step instruction and practical tips on how to create Web site indexes using various kinds of software. Aimed at experienced and novice indexers, this book focuses on hyperlinked back-of-the-book style indexes for Web sites, intranets, or subsites. I have provided more detailed instruction than available elsewhere on the use of all the various software packages for the creation of Web site indexes, including the HTML output options of dedicated book indexing software.

The book starts with an overview of HTML codes both for hyperlinks and for various methods to create indented subentries. I also discuss choice of content and term development specific to Web site indexes. This particular aspect of Web indexing has not been covered in other publications. The final chapter includes information on the freelance market and provides marketing tips for freelancers seeking to work on Web site indexing.

While acknowledging that the field of "Web indexing" is broad in scope, I have purposely kept the scope of this book narrower so I could focus on a practical "how-to" approach. The larger field of Web indexing also includes such topics as converting a printed book index to a hyperlinked Web site index, indexing online help, creating a Web-based database index, and indexing Web pages with metadata keywords for search engine retrieval. Each of these topics is worthy of its own treatise, just as the subject of how to create hyperlinked Web site indexes is able to fill a book. I also chose to write this book as a single author rather than follow the format of other ASI publications that uses multiple contributors. By having the viewpoint of one author, the explanations flow more cohesively and have uniformity in style and purpose.

This book meets a need that has not been satisfied although two books have previously been published in the field of Web indexing. Glenda Browne and Jon Jermey's book *Website Indexing: Enhancing Access to Information Within Websites* (Auslib Press, 2004) takes a broader approach to the field of Web indexing and thus provides fewer step-by-step instructions on the specific topic of creating hyperlinked A–Z indexes. James Lamb's self-published book *Website Indexes: Visitors to Content in Two Clicks* (Jalamb.com Ltd, 2006), on the other hand, has an even narrower scope, since it is devoted to only one software tool, XRefHT.

I have offered a series of online Web site indexing courses since 2005. Readers of this book may wonder whether they should also take these courses. While the online courses include exercises that are not part of this book, as well as, most significantly, live links to Web site indexes and other resources on the Web, the major difference is that the course provides participants with feedback on their work and the opportunity to participate in a dedicated discussion group. Past or current course students may wonder if it is also worth buying this book. This book encompasses the content of all of the courses or modules (with the exception of related topics of database, taxonomies, and metadata indexing) and will serve as a companion reference work for the courses. The online workshop offered through Simmons College Graduate School of Library and Information Science Continuing Education program is actually a shortened course, covering about half of the material discussed in this book. The book also has additional sections, such as the history of Web site indexing, and material updated since fall 2006. For those who have only read the material online, print documentation makes a ready reference while working on a Web site index at the computer.

Writing the book has allowed me to be comprehensive in a way that neither online discussion nor class lecture has. This book includes instructions on a number of software programs. Some of them I use routinely while others rarely. Although I have made every attempt to be accurate and thorough, it is still possible that I have overlooked a helpful feature or procedure related to one or more of the programs. My purpose here is to give sufficient information so you can at least get started creating Web site indexes with the software tool of your choice. I have tested my directions and know that they work, but there may be other shortcuts or methods that more experienced users of the software know and can apply to get the same results.

At the time I was considering a career in freelance indexing, I was also considering a career in Web site design or information architecture. Web site indexing allowed me to combine both of these interests. I do take on back-of-the-book indexing, but Web site indexing is just more fun to do and provides diversity in my work. At the time of this writing, the demand for freelance Web site indexing is slowly growing, and it is my belief that the more people there are who can offer such services, the greater the awareness and subsequent demand will be for Web indexes. Because there has not been adequate specialized training for Web site indexing, many of the existing Web site indexes suffer from poor quality. It is my hope that the more high-quality Web site indexes become available, the more they will be appreciated and requested by Web site owners. Therefore, those of us who index Web sites welcome more indexers into our ranks.

As I mentioned already, I am not a regular user of all the types of software that I discuss in Chapter 4. I wish to acknowledge feedback and corrections from the various vendors and representatives of the major types of dedicated indexing software: Gale Rhoades for taking the time to explain HTML indexing in Macrex, Kamm Schreiner for his comments on SKY Index Professional, and David Ream for his feedback on using HTML/Prep with CINDEX. Going beyond her company's own software tools, Gale also helped me understand the distinction between outputting an HTML index and converting a book index to HTML, and Kamm made it clear to me that a URL can be entered into any field of the book indexing software.

I also wish to acknowledge Seth Maislin, who first got me interested in back-of-the-book style indexing, Kevin Broccoli for teaching me the basics of Web site indexing, Dwight Walker for sharing with me the history of Web site indexing and for making me aware of Tim Craven and his XRefHT freeware, and James Lamb for inspiring me to write a book on Web indexing by his own recent example. Until I read James's explanations, I was not aware of all of XRefHT's features, such as its capability in converting indexes. I greatly appreciated Tim Craven's presentation on XRefHT at last year's ASI conference at my request and his answering of subsequent questions. Marilyn Rowland and Diane Brenner, editors of *Beyond Book Indexing* and prior officers of my ASI chapter (New England), have served as professional models for me. If I had not known the editors of that volume personally, I might not have endeavored to follow in their footsteps and write a new ASI book. More than just an acknowledgment, but a great big thanks goes to ASI Publications Chair Enid Zafran for accepting my book proposal and tirelessly editing every page in detail. Finally, I thank ASI and Web Indexing SIG member Linda Kenny Sloan for writing the index of this book.

—Heather Hedden

Chapter 1

Introduction to Web Site Indexes

INTRODUCTION

An index is a tool to help people find specific desired information within a document or set of documents. Although originally designed for printed material, the same type of index used in books or periodicals can be applied to electronic documents or Web pages, and it can be similarly effective.

The main reason why we do not see more back-of-the-book-style indexes on Web sites and intranets is not because such indexes are not suitable to Web pages, but rather because these sites often offer other means of searching. Most significantly they rely on search engines, which range from simple, free software applications to complex, custom-programmed solutions. Finding information on Web sites may also be done through multilevel (dropdown) navigation menus, searchable databases with faceted browsing, site maps, or other tools. Despite the competition from these other searching/finding methods, which are discussed in more detail later, a well-written index on many sites often provides the most effective searching method.

Another reason why we do not see more Web site indexes is that the tools and techniques to create them are not well known. While well-established software products and courses of instruction exist for back-of-the-book indexing, few professional indexers and even fewer Web professionals know of Web indexing software or simply how to begin Web site indexing. The literature on Web site information architecture (how to structurally design large Web sites) might mention that site indexes are a good idea, but give no explanation of exactly how to do it. The best known book on information architecture, *Information Architecture for the World Wide Web* by Peter Morville and Louis Rosenfeld (2nd Edition, O'Reilly, 2002) includes screenshot examples of Web site indexes and offers the following explanation:

Search [engines] may be a good way to serve your site's users, but other ways may work better. For example, if you don't have the technical expertise or confidence to configure a search engine or the money to shell out for one, consider providing a site index instead. Both site indexes and search engines help users who know what they're looking for. While a site index can be a heck of a lot of work, it is typically created and maintained manually, and can therefore be maintained by anyone who knows HTML. (p. 133)

Morville and Rosenfeld make no mention in their book of any software to aid in Web site indexing. Yet, by using various software, indexing a Web site presents no more work than indexing a similar-sized book. Furthermore, knowledge of HTML (hypertext markup language), while highly recommended, is actually not necessary, since the indexing software or HTML editing software takes care of generating the HTML code. Knowledge of indexing techniques, though, is needed to create a usable Web site index, although a lower level of indexing is needed to merely maintain the index.

This book is intended to serve the purpose of making the tools and techniques for Web site indexing better known to indexers, aspiring indexers, Web site professionals, and Web site owners.

WEB SITE A–Z INDEXES DEFINED

The terms "Web site indexes" and "Web site indexing" can have various meanings. Thus, for clarification, the types of Web site indexes on which this book focuses may be called "Web site A–Z indexes." The use of "A–Z" terminology implies that there is an alphabetical browse view or interface. This interface differs from that of a browse through layers of hierarchical categories (also known as a taxonomy), which, although not necessarily alphabetical, are also found on some Web sites. The A–Z index is also different from a behind-the-scenes index that involves a search box. Even if terms entered into the search box are matched against a human-created index, thesaurus, or controlled vocabulary, these terms are not visible to the user and therefore not browsable.

Although an A–Z index could be used to index multiple sites rather than the multiple pages of a single site, this rarely happens. When multiple sites are organized, they tend to fall into categories rather than into alphabetical indexes. Therefore, this book will focus on A–Z indexes for single Web sites or intranets, or merely portions of sites.

The A–Z index itself often constitutes just a single page within a Web site. But if the index is long, it may be segmented into multiple pages, such as one Web page for the entries that start with each letter of the alphabet or for a limited range of letters of the alphabet, such as A–C, D–F, and so on. As such, an A–Z index is simpler to create than a taxonomy, which requires multiple Web pages, one for each level of the hierarchy. A browsable A–Z index is also simpler to create than a searchable thesaurus, which may require a database or some level of programming.

On Web sites, A–Z indexes are typically given various titles, listed in order of popularity as found on Google:

- Site index
- A–Z index
- Topic index
- Alphabetical index
- Browsable index

WEB SITE INDEX STRUCTURE

The Web site A–Z index as defined here follows the structure of indexes commonly found at the back of books. The browsable alphabetical index is a style with which users are familiar. Certain modifications need to be made, however, to adapt the index to the Web.

Hypertext Instead of Page Number Locators

In book indexes, entries or subentries are followed by one or more page numbers (locators), referring the reader to the page of the book with the topic of the index entry. In a Web site index, there are typically no page numbers. Instead, the text of the entry or subentry itself is hyperlinked to the target page within the Web site where the topic is discussed.

A complication with Web site indexes arises because a hyperlink can go to only one destination. So, by relying on the hyperlink of the text of the entry as the means of jumping to the source content, you cannot have multiple locators as you may have a series of page numbers following an index entry when the same topic appears on multiple pages. Having hyperlinked page numbers following the entry is a possibility, but the page numbers themselves become rather meaningless in a Web site. Thus, it is not so common to see them in Web site indexes, except in the instance of books posted on the Web. To get around this problem of multiple locators in Web site indexes, such as creating additional subentries or sub-subentries, see the discussion in Chapter 8.

Not only do print indexes use multiple page numbers after many entries, but they also have page ranges, such as 67–70. Page ranges also present a problem in hypertext, although they do not seriously affect Web site indexes due to the structure of the sites. If several pages of a Web site all discuss the same topic, then they are likely to be subpages of an intermediate page introducing that section of the Web site. The index then can link to the intermediate page. Also, Web sites have no restriction on page length, so if there is a lengthy discussion on one topic, it may flow continuously in a single, lengthy page. The general design of Web sites follows the rule of one Web page for each topic, no matter the length of the page.

Thus, the nature of traditional Web sites makes them relatively easy to index with a single locator/link per entry. Web sites that are collections of articles, however, present more of a challenge. But these issues really mirror similar issues in print indexing, such as creating a cumulative index to periodical articles instead of an index to a book, narrative, or monograph.

Hypertext locators also have an advantage over page numbers. Instead of pointing to an entire page, index entries can be more precise by linking to specific points (sections, paragraphs, etc.) within a page. This is done by inserting a kind of HTML tag known as a "named anchor" to target a certain point within the page. The named anchors may already occur in the Web pages, but often the indexer may feel the need to add more. Inserting named anchors requires the indexer to go beyond just writing the index itself. In many Web sites, where the pages are not unusually long, creating index entries that point to an entire page rather than a more specific anchor point may suffice.

Not every entry in an index is hypertext and thus linked. If there is a main entry with multiple subentries, the main entry often is not linked to any pages, but serves as a gathering point for the subentries. This is the same style as in book indexing, where a main entry has no page locators. In the following example, the main entry "intranets" has no locators in either the book index excerpt on the left or in the Web site index on the right:

intranets	intranets
content management and, 13	<u>content management and</u>
history of, 12	<u>history of</u>
indexing of, 43	<u>indexing of</u>

The most common way to make it clear to the user which entries are hyperlinked to content and which are not is to use different colors and to underline the linkable phrases.

Cross-References

See cross-references are used in print indexes as an alternative to "double posting," typically when synonymous main entries have many subentries. They save space by making it unnecessary to repeat all the subentries. On Web sites, the issue of space disappears. The *See* cross-references are, therefore, less often used for this purpose. Instead, all equivalent terms, no matter how many subentries they have, tend to be entered.

Another purpose of a *See* reference is to educate the user as to the preferred term. There is no need, however, to make the user jump somewhere else within the index before going to the source text, if there are no subentries. In a Web site index, the

See reference names the preferred term, but it may link directly to the source text rather than to the location of the referred term within the index. For example, in the entry **Personnel.** *See* **Human Resources**, the term **Human Resources** is hyperlinked to the page about Human Resources and not to the entry **Human Resources** within the index.

See also cross-references are as helpful in Web indexes as they are in print indexes. Their purpose in both cases is to guide users to related terms that may offer additional tangential information on a topic. In a Web site index, the referring term is hyperlinked to jump to the referred term within the index or directly to the page with the content, depending on the existence of subentries. Web site index cross-references are explained in more detail in Chapter 7.

Letters for Navigation

Whether a Web site index takes one page or falls across multiple pages, the standard method of navigating the entire index, which exceeds the size of one screen, is to have the letters of the alphabet displayed at the top of the page and have the letters hyperlinked to the section of the index that begins with that letter of the alphabet.

The letters of the alphabet may be displayed at the top of the index or each index page only, or also at the bottom of pages and in between letters, or in a separate frame that is always visible.

There is also a choice of style as to whether all the letters of the alphabet are displayed, including those for which there are no index entries, such as X, or to list only letters for which there are index entries. If there are no index entries for a letter, then the letter is simply not hyperlinked. Since it therefore does not display in link color or is underlined, it should be clear to the user no entries exist under this letter. In the following example, letters with no index entries are grayed out:

<u>A</u> <u>B</u> <u>C</u> <u>D</u> <u>E</u> <u>F</u> <u>G</u> <u>H</u> <u>I</u> <u>J</u> <u>K</u> <u>L</u> <u>M</u> <u>N</u> <u>O</u> <u>P</u> Q <u>R</u> <u>S</u> <u>T</u> <u>U</u> V <u>W</u> X <u>Y</u> Z

When an index page is long, occasional "Back to Top" or "Top of Page" jump links also provide useful aids to users. These directional links may be inserted after each letter section or after multiple letter sections if the sections are short.

TYPES OF WEB SITE INDEXES

Even within the narrow definition of Web site A–Z indexes, we find various kinds:

1. Indexes of book-like documents that are on Web sites or intranets or ebooks
2. Indexes of entire Web sites or subsites
3. Periodical indexes that are online or newsletter sections of Web sites

6   Indexing Specialties: Web Sites

Indexes of Book-Like Documents

Indexing book-like documents within Web sites or intranets or as ebooks follows book indexing practices. Entries and subentries tend to be hyperlinked (by use of named anchors) to section headings within Web pages, rather than to just the top of the page. Web pages tend to be of consistent lengths, and section headings usually have anchors. While these types of Web indexes are perhaps the easiest to index for experienced book indexers, they are unfortunately not commonly found. Existing indexes of book-type documents on the Web sometimes follow book indexing style so closely that page numbers are retained and cross-references are not even hyperlinked.

An example of a book with an index with retained page numbers on the Web is the book *Reminiscences and Memoirs of North Carolina and Eminent North Carolinians* by John H. Wheeler at www.researchonline.net/nccw/bios/wheeler.htm (Figure 1.1).

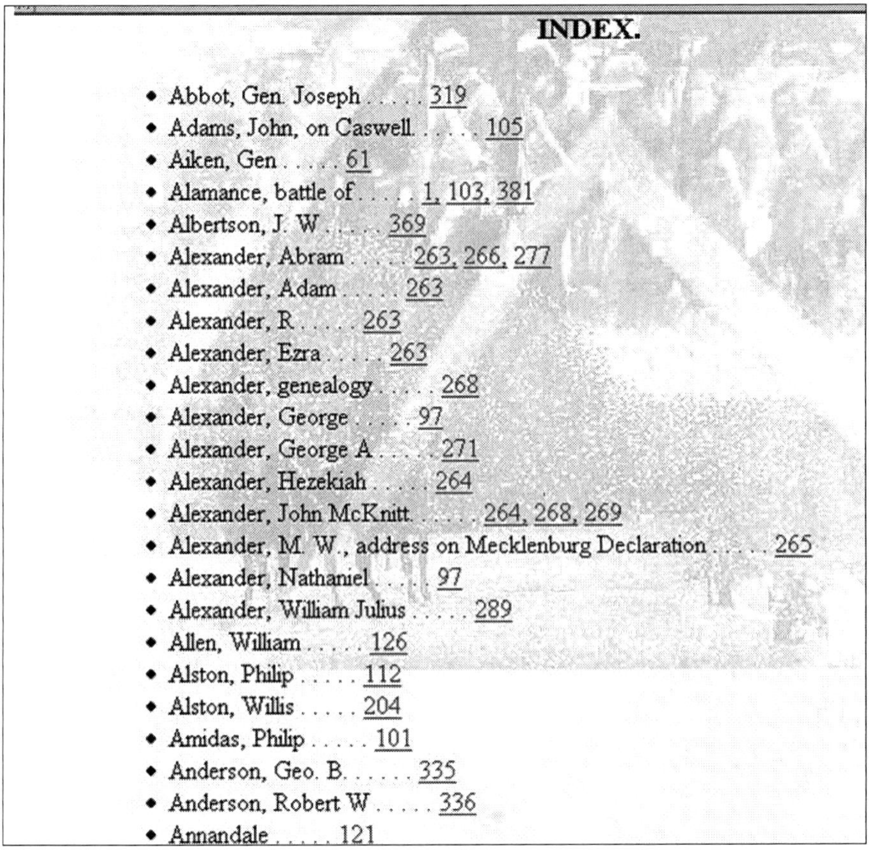

INDEX.

- Abbot, Gen. Joseph 319
- Adams, John, on Caswell 105
- Aiken, Gen 61
- Alamance, battle of 1, 103, 381
- Albertson, J. W. 369
- Alexander, Abram 263, 266, 277
- Alexander, Adam 263
- Alexander, R 263
- Alexander, Ezra 263
- Alexander, genealogy 268
- Alexander, George 97
- Alexander, George A 271
- Alexander, Hezekiah 264
- Alexander, John McKnitt 264, 268, 269
- Alexander, M. W., address on Mecklenburg Declaration 265
- Alexander, Nathaniel 97
- Alexander, William Julius 289
- Allen, William 126
- Alston, Philip 112
- Alston, Willis 204
- Amidas, Philip 101
- Anderson, Geo. B. 335
- Anderson, Robert W 336
- Annandale 121

Figure 1.1

Introduction to Web Site Indexes 7

Indexes of Entire Web Sites

Indexes of entire Web sites also resemble book indexes, but the indexer needs to take into consideration the perspectives and goals of different users of the Web site. These could include employees, members, visitors, customers, prospective customers, and so forth. While readers of books and their indexes are seeking information, users of Web sites may not only want information, but may also want to perform a task, such as purchase a product, register for a program, or download software. The index entries also need to take into consideration such task-oriented needs. Sometimes it makes more sense to create separate indexes for separate sections of a Web site, if different sections serve different users with different purposes. Page length within Web sites can vary greatly, and section headings may lack anchors, requiring the indexer to insert them or to request their insertion by the site's owner.

An example of a general Web site index is on the site of the American Society of Indexers at www.asindexing.org/site/backndx.htm (Figure 1.2). Note that the navigational letters at the top are in a separate frame and that members-area links are indicated with asterisks.

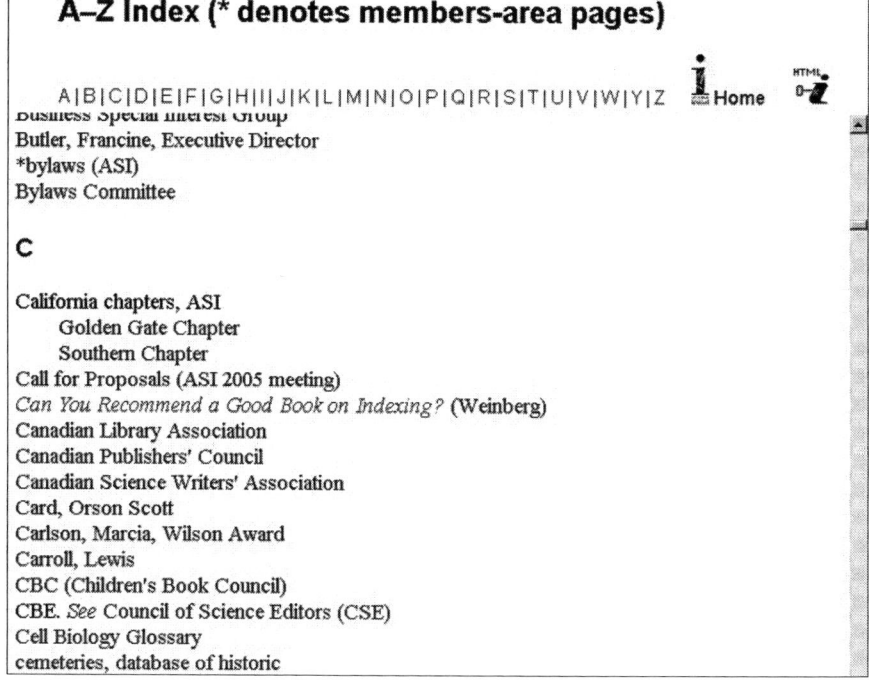

Figure 1.2

8 Indexing Specialties: Web Sites

Periodical Indexes

Periodical indexes include a growing number of traditional print periodicals that now offer some of their articles on their Web sites. There are also organizations that put periodic newsletter articles on their Web sites. Finally, some Web sites consist mostly of articles, such as the sites of zines or blogs.

In all of these cases, Web indexes tend not to be done of the entire Web site (not the home page, contact page, etc.), but rather are created just for the articles. This type of indexing resembles journal indexing. Indexing tends to be done to the level of the article, not more specifically. On the Web, no matter how long (how many words) an article is, it occupies just a single Web page; indexing occurs at the level of the Web page and usually not to sections within the pages. Thus, inserting and linking index entries to anchors is not common.

In article collections, there tends to be more than one article on the same subject over time. In a Web index, since each entry can point/link to only one location, a date may need to be included as part of the entry to differentiate it.

An example of a periodical index can be found at the Web site of *Consumer Reports* magazine (www.consumerreports.org) (Figure 1.3).

Figure 1.3

HISTORY OF WEB INDEXING

Although individuals skilled in both indexing and HTML coding have experimented with creating Web site indexes from the start of the Web in the early- to mid-1990s, the field of creating A–Z site indexes was formally started in Australia. In 1995, Australian indexer and PC trainer Jonathan Jermey developed the first Windows program specifically for converting indexes into HTML, freeware called Weblinkr. Around that time, DOS index conversion utilities were also developed: HTML/Prep by Leverage Technologies in the United States and INDTOHTM freeware by Canadian information science professor Timothy Craven. The Webmaster of the Australian Society of Indexers (AusSi) at the time, Dwight Walker, took on the promotion of the software and the field of Web indexing. In 1996, he bundled and distributed a group of tools he dubbed WEBIX, which included Weblinkr for Windows, INDTOHTM for DOS, plus Netscape and notes on Web indexing. Walker, a PC trainer and programmer himself, later designed his own version of WEBIX, which he did not release due to subsequent competition from the program HTML Indexer released by David Brown of Brown Inc. in the United States in 1998. Craven continued to work on his Web indexing freeware. He later came out with a dedicated Windows Web indexing freeware program called XRefHT32, which he continues to update. In 2006, Craven released a cross-platform Java version of XRefHT.

Also back in 1996, Walker, along with Maureen Henninger, an information science lecturer at the University of New South Wales, and Kerry Webb of the Australian Library and Information Association (ALIA) started up the Australian Society of Indexers (AusSI) Web Indexing Prize with the aim of encouraging indexers to learn how to create Web site indexes. The prize was first awarded in 1996 and was awarded every year through 2000, after which it was replaced by a reward system that is more of an endorsement. The initial 1996 winner was the Webmaster for the library of the Parliament of Australia. Subsequent prize winners have been both Australian and international. Recipients are listed at www.aussi.org/prizes/webindex awards.htm.

Shortly thereafter, Henninger started teaching the first course in Web indexing, a one-day continuing education workshop at the University of New South Wales, which was offered intermittently through 2003. The workshop was discontinued only when the University of New South Wales decided to no longer offer any continuing education workshops. Meanwhile, Walker created and taught the first online training course in Web site indexing for several months in 1998, which attracted students in the United States, Canada, and the United Kingdom. Walker discontinued his workshop due to competition from his former student Kevin Broccoli in the United States, who began offering his own online course. Broccoli continued offering his online course until he redirected the focus of his business away from indexing in 2004. One of his former students, Heather Hedden (the author of this book), began offering a new online course in 2005. The following year, a condensed online workshop started being offered through Simmons College Graduate School of Library and Information Science Continuing Education program.

Australian indexers and Web experts Jonathan Jermey and Glenda Browne (in cooperation with Henninger) used the University of New South Wales workshop notes, along with articles they had each published in the Australian information science journal *Online Currents*, as a basis for writing the first book devoted to Web indexing, *Website Indexing: Enhancing Access to Information Within Websites*, which was published by Auslib Press in 2001. A second edition was published in 2004.

Web indexing first appeared as a topic at an American Society of Indexers (ASI) conference in Seattle, Washington, in 1998. Walker traveled from Australia to the conference and led a roundtable session on Web indexing. Another roundtable on indexing Web documents was led by Gerry Van Ravenswaay. The 1999 ASI conference in Indianapolis, Indiana, included the first full-day workshop in the U.S. on Web site indexing. It was jointly led by Broccoli, Van Ravenswaay, and Marilyn Rowland. Workshops or other sessions on aspects of Web indexing have been presented at most ASI conferences since then. Broccoli, Rowland, and Van Ravenswaay, among other ASI members, then contributed to the ASI/Information Today, Inc. book, *Beyond Book Indexing: How to Get Started in Web Indexing, Embedded Indexing, and Other Computer-Based Media*, which was published in 2000 with Rowland and Diane Brenner as editors.

It was also at the ASI 1998 conference that the ASI Web Indexing Special Interest Group (SIG) was first established. The SIG, led by Broccoli and Van Ravenswaay, created its own Web site and an online discussion group. Due to lack of volunteer efforts, the SIG gradually became inactive. It was reactivated again in January 2005 under the leadership of Heather Hedden. A new affiliated discussion group, hosted on Yahoo!, also started at that time.

Another approach to Web indexing has been by means of indexing online help, which is often output as HTML. Indexers leading in this area have included Jan C. Wright, who led an ASI conference workshop on the subject in 1998, and Bill Meisheid, who led a conference workshop in 1999. Wright also published an article on online indexing in *The Indexer* as early as 1997, and Meisheid published a book on indexing with RoboHelp HTML Edition in 2001.

The latest book on Web indexing, *Website Indexes: Visitors to Content in Two Clicks,* was written in 2006 by James Lamb, a member of the Society of Indexers in the United Kingdom. The book focuses on how to create indexes with Tim Craven's freeware XRefHT32. The idea for writing that book came from discussion originating on the Web Indexing SIG's Yahoo! discussion group.

Web site indexing today is still not an established field. The majority of Web site indexes are still created by Webmasters untrained in indexing and unaware of the existence of trained freelance Web site indexers. It is hoped that indexers and their professional associations will do more to educate the Web development community in the availability of trained Web indexers and other resources in Web site indexing.

FURTHER READING

Brenner, Diane and Marilyn Rowland. *Beyond Book Indexing: How to Get Started in Web Indexing, Embedded Indexing, and Other Computer-Based Media*. Medford, NJ: Information Today, Inc., 2000.

Browne, Glenda and Jonathan Jermey. *Website Indexing: Enhancing Access to Information Within Websites*, 2nd Edition. Adelaide, South Australia: Auslib Press, 2004. Available at www.lulu.com/content/331919.

Lamb, James A. *Website Indexes: Visitors to Content in Two Clicks*. Ardleigh, Essex, England: Jalamb.com Ltd., 2006. Available at www.lulu.com/content/300848.

Meisheid, William. *Successful Indexing With RoboHELP HTML Edition*. Ellicott City, MD: Sageline Publishing, 2001.

Rosenfeld, Louis and Peter Morville. *Information Architecture for the World Wide Web*, 2nd Edition. Sebastopol, CA: O'Reilly & Associates, 2002.

Chapter 2

HTML Basics

INTRODUCTION TO HTML

One of the reasons why so few people index Web sites is that many indexers do not feel comfortable working in HTML. However, HTML is not that difficult to learn. In fact, you need to learn only some to create Web site indexes, and software can take care of all of it anyway.

HTML stands for hypertext markup language. Hypertext is specially designated text (i.e., underlined and/or in a different color) that when clicked on causes the Web browser to load a new Web page or a different section of the existing page. Thus, it is text that is designated as a "link." Although HTML gets its name from the hypertext linking feature, the HTML coding language deals with much more than just the text used for links. It is not even limited to text, but also encompasses how to handle graphics.

This isn't coding, as done by programmers. Rather, certain tags are used, usually in pairs both before and after a piece of text, to indicate to the Web browser that the text should be displayed in a certain way and/or that the text should have hypertext link capability. The tags are to "mark up" the text, hence the name "markup language." It is more appropriate to compare this to the field of copyediting and the use of standard copyediting marks.

You do not need special software to create HTML pages. The pages consist of pure text that you can type in a simple text editor, such as Notepad in Windows or SimpleText in Mac. While entire Web sites can be created by typing all the codes in a text editor—and a few people still do it that way—most people today use an HTML editing program. This way you don't have to learn or remember all the HTML codes. And even if you did, the HTML editing software removes the tedium of typing all the tags. It gives you a WYSIWYG ("what you see is what you get") display as the Web pages are being created. It essentially works like a special word processor.

With the availability of HTML editing programs, why then learn any HTML?

- It's important to recognize the tags when you see them, so that you can find your way around within the code view of a Web page if necessary.

13

- You may need to understand and change some tags "by hand," when you cannot get the HTML editing software to do exactly what you want it to do. For example, you may have difficulty placing the cursor in the correct place between two pieces of text that are coded differently.
- As a Web site indexer, you might be asked to format the index page, unlike the case for printed indexes.
- When it comes to Web site indexes, if you want to make a minor change in an already formatted index, it is sometimes preferred to do so in HTML code rather than through the HTML editing software to make sure you do not unintentionally change the indented formatting.
- As a Web site indexer, you might also be asked to assign keywords to Web pages in the descriptor meta tag field, so you should know what that is and where to find it.
- If you see some aspect of Web page design (namely formatting, not copyrighted text) that you like in another Web site, you can copy and paste snippets of the HTML code into your own Web page.

The following sections provide an overview of basic HTML tags. Chapter 3 then addresses HTML and HTML Editor use specific to Web site indexes.

BASIC HTML TAGS

HTML tags are instructions that appear within angle brackets (< >). Most often, the instructions also come in pairs, one at the beginning of the designated text and another with a slash inserted (</ >) at the end of the designated text, to "turn off" the code instruction. These paired tags are also known as "container" tags. Here is an example:

```
<b>Text to be bolded</b>
```

As you may have guessed, <b> is the HTML tag to make text bold. The text will be bolded up to the </b> tag, which stops bolding.

This list gives a few more basic formatting tags:

- `<p> </p>` – paragraph (a blank line appears between paragraphs)
- `<i> </i>` – italics
- `<u> </u>` – underline (avoid so as not to confuse with hypertext)
- `<strong> </strong>` – same as bold
- `<h1> </h1>` – heading level #1, etc. (up to h6)
- `<blockquote> </blockquote>` – indents the paragraph on both sides

When using multiple tags on the same piece of text, keep them properly nested from inside to out. For example, either of the following will work:

```
<i><b>sample text</b></i> OR <b><i>sample text</i></b>
```

but never the following, which will not work:

```
<b><i>sample text</b></i> OR <i><b>sample text</i></b>
```

There are a few tags that do not come in pairs, and are known as "empty" tags. For example, the line break code of <br>:

```
After this text there is a line break.<br>
```

There is also HTML code for special characters or spaces that does not even require the brackets. An example is the code for a space. In HTML, only a single space between words within text is recognized. If you want to create more consecutive spaces, perhaps for stylistic reasons, you must type the code ** ** to indicate "nonbreaking space." Thus two spaces between two words are written as:

```
text  text
```

Tags for the Basic Web Page

A Web page is based on a single HTML document or file. (A "Web site" refers to multiple Web pages that are linked together by an introductory page designated as the home page.) What makes the document HTML is the tag <html> at the start of the document. The tag </html> concludes the document.

In every Web page, there is a part of the page that is displayed in the browser and a part that is not displayed but contains more general information about the page. The displayed section is called the Body and the non-displayed, general information section is called the Head.

The HTML coding structure of a Web page follows the template:

```
<html>
    <head>
        (Various non-displayed head information goes
        here.)
    </head>
    <body>
        (The body or the displayed text of the Web page
        goes here.)
    </body>
</html>
```

Basic principles for HTML tags include the following:

- HTML tag pairs are nested within each other. The outside pair of tags are <html> </html>, and "nested" within this pair are two more pairs of tags for the Head and Body sections. Additional pairs of tags lie within the Head section or within the Body section of the page.
- In code, line breaks, indents, and spaces (other than a single space between words in text) do not matter and are not displayed. In writing code, line breaks and indents are often used merely to make the coded text easier to read.
- Capitalization of the tag designation within the angle brackets does not matter. Tags of <HTML>, <HEAD>, <B> work the same as <html>, <head>, and <b>.

Tags with Descriptive Attributes

Tags with a single letter or word within the angle brackets are the simplest HTML tags. But designing and formatting Web pages involves a lot of descriptive attributes, such as background color, text alignment, font style, size, color, and so on. All this descriptive information also goes within the angle-bracket tags. Descriptive attributes appear in quotes following an equal sign (=), following the wording for the attribute type. Here are some examples of tags indicating fonts:

```
<font color="red">sample text</font>
<font face="Arial, Helvetica, sans-serif">sample text</font>
<font size="2">sample text</font>
```

Also, a combination of attributes may be included within one set of tags:

```
<font color="#FF9900" size="2" face="Courier New, Courier, mono">sample text</font>
```

Although basic colors may be described by words, it is more precise to choose from the 256 different colors for which 6-digit (or hexadecimal) alphanumeric codes are used, such as <font color="#FF9900">. Note that font face will often include a list of three fonts as similar alternatives, depending on what fonts the user's browser supports, such as ="Arial, Helvetica, sans-serif." The fonts available for text in Web sites are very limited. Likewise, font sizes are relative to the default, and not given in absolute pixel sizes, since the ultimate appearance of the font depends on the user's browser.

Tags with descriptive attributes, such as for text alignment, text color, or background color, can be used for a paragraph or for the entire body of the Web page, as in the following examples:

```
<p align="center">
<body bgcolor="blue" text="#FF9900">
```

Note again that any number of attributes can be included within the body tags.

Tags for Tables

Formatting text or other content on a Web site into columns, in boxes, alongside images, and in any other special way is typically done by creating tables. Tables are not used within Web site indexes, but a Web site index might be placed within a page that uses a table for overall page formatting. In that case the index might be nested within one large cell/column within a table, with a navigation menu located within another cell/column.

The tables and their rows and columns can be formatted for height, width, cell spacing and padding, cell borders, background color, and the alignment of content within the cells. Creating tables without using HTML editing software can be tricky, so I will not go into all the details here. The examples that follow serve simply for the purposes of recognition.

To designate a column the entire length (100%) of the page and occupying one-quarter of the width, the code might be:

```
<table width="25%" height="100%" border="0" cell spacing="2">
```

For a table cell or column within a table, the code <td> is used for "table data":

```
<td width="424" valign="top">
```

Note that width and height may be designated either in pixels or in percentage of the display. You do not need to specify width and/or height, though, leaving the table cells to expand around the cell content. The attribute "valign" refers to vertical alignment. Vertical alignment options are top, middle, or bottom.

Tables also use the code <tr> for table row, which does not contain any descriptive value. All table codes are container codes, so at the end of a cell is the code </td>, at the end of a row is the code </tr>, and at the end of the table is the code </table>.

Tags for Images

Images are occasionally inserted into indexes, such as arrows to link back to the top of the page or icons next to index entries to indicate something (such as a padlock icon for password restricted access or a PDF document icon to indicate that the page is a PDF file). Images are added to Web pages with the tag designation of "img." Following the tag, you must provide the name of the image file, known as the source file (which also must be uploaded to the Web server). For example:

```
<img src="logo.gif">
```

This means that the image of the file named logo.gif should appear on this place in the page. The image tag is not a container tag. It simply inserts an image wherever the descriptive tag is placed. Image files most often employ the extensions .gif or .jpg. Additional file location, description, and image dimension information can optionally be included:

```
<img src="images/logo.gif" alt="Information Logo"
width="80" height="80">
```

In this case, the file named logo.gif is located in the images folder of the Web site. The text specified by "alt=" will appear if the user's browser graphics are disabled or when the user mouses over the image. The specified dimensions of the image enable the user's browser to load the Web page more quickly.

HEAD CONTENT TAGS
Tags for the Page Title

There are different types of optional content that can go into the Head section of a Web page. The most important of these is the title of the page. Do not confuse this with the name of the file, which must not contain spaces and must end in .htm or .html. The title can use any characters and can consist of several words with spaces in between. Thus, it can be a little longer and more accurate than the file name. Since what appears in the Head section does not display in the Web page, the title may be repeated within the body, typically within heading tags, such as h2 in this example.

Here is an example of a title within a Web page:

```
<html>
    <head>
        <title>Site A-Z Index</title>
    <head>
    <body>
        <h2>Site A-Z Index</h2>
        <p>text</p>
    <body>
<html>
```

While the title does not display in the Web page, it does display in other important places. These include in the title bar of the Web browser at the very top of the screen, which is above the browser's menu, and in the displayed page title result from a search engine retrieval.

Metadata Tags

Metadata literally means data about data. It is information about the Web page. Taking an analogy from the book/library world, metadata resembles the bibliographic or cataloging information. The metadata on the home page may also be considered as the metadata for the entire Web site. Metadata, indicated in meta tags, is located within the Head portion of a Web page. There are numerous possible meta tags. Some sites have many and some have none. Meta tags are not necessary, but I recommend you use at least the meta tags for Description and Keywords.

Since meta tags are not container tags, they require no closing tag. All the information they refer to falls within the paired angle-bracket code. The meta tags have not only an attribute, but also have content information. The Description meta tag is as follows:

```
<meta name="description" content="A description of the
Web page here.">
```

As part of the Head content, the Description is not displayed in the web page. The Description is what displays in search engine retrieval results for web sites. In search results, in addition to the title of the page, there is usually a short description of the site, and this description comes from the meta tag. The words in the Description meta tag are also taken into account when the search engine "searches" for Web sites to match the word(s) a user typed into the search box.

The Keywords meta tag appears as follows:

```
<meta name="keywords" content="keyword1, keyword2, key
phrase">
```

The Keywords meta tag is similar to the Description meta tag. Multiple keywords or multiple-word phrases are listed with commas separating them. You can have any number of keywords. Meta tag Keywords, like words in the Description, are used for search engine retrieval of Web sites or by a search engine on a site to retrieve individual Web site pages. Meta tag Keywords can play a role in human indexing of Web sites as well, when keywords are assigned consistently to all pages across a Web site.

TAGS FOR LISTS

Different sets of tags can be used for creating indented lists of text. These are useful for indexers to know as a means to format indented subentries. Chapter 3 will cover other methods of creating indented subentries.

There are three kinds of HTML lists:

1. Ordered lists, which are numbered

2. Unordered lists, which are bulleted
3. Definition lists, which comprise entries and their "definitions"

Ordered Lists

The previous list is an example of an ordered list. Here is its code:

```
<ol>
   <li>Ordered lists, which are numbered</li>
   <li>Unordered lists, which are bulleted</li>
   <li>Definition lists, which comprise entries and their
   "definitions"</li>
</ol>
```

`<ol>` starts the ordered list and `</ol>` ends the ordered list. `<li>` starts a list item and `</li>` ends a list item.

Unordered Lists

An unordered list is a bulleted list, such as the following example:

- Ordered lists, which are numbered
- Unordered lists, which are bulleted
- Definition lists, which comprise entries and their "definitions"

Here is the code for the unordered list above:

```
<ul>
    <li>Ordered lists, which are numbered</li>
    <li>Unordered lists, which are bulleted</li>
    <li> Definition lists, which comprise entries and
    their "definitions"</li>
</ul>
```

`<ul>` starts the unordered list, and `</ul>` ends the unordered list. `<li>` starts a list item, and `</li>` ends a list item.

Definition Lists

Definition lists present more of a challenge, because they have two components, a "term" and a "definition." One or more definitions appear under a term. Here is an example:

> Ordered lists
> > which are numbered

Unordered lists
> which are bulleted

Definition lists
> which comprise entries and their "definitions"

Here is the code for the above text:

```
<dl>
    <dt>Ordered lists</dt>
        <dd>which are numbered</dd>
    <dt>Unordered lists</dt>
        <dd>which are bulleted</dd>
    <dt>Definition lists</dt>
        <dd>which comprise entries and their
        "definitions"</dd>
</dl>
```

`<dl>` starts the definition list, and `</dl>` ends the definition list. `<dt>` starts a definition-list term, and `</dt>` ends a definition-list term. `<dd>` starts a definition-list definition, and `</dd>` ends a definition-list definition.

For all three of these list types, sets of codes may be nested within each other to create lists within lists.

TAGS FOR LINKS

HTML links are of four main kinds:

1. **Internal links, also known as "jump links"** – These link from one place to another place within the same page. These tend to be utilized for longer Web pages.
2. **Links between pages within a Web site** – These links are absolutely necessary to create a Web site.
3. **External links to other Web sites** – These are what make the World Wide Web what it is—a Web of Web sites linked to each other.
4. **E-mail (mailto) links** – These are not used in indexes.

There are also combinations of links, such as to specific places within a different page.

Both internal links and links between pages are necessary for creating alphabetical Web site indexes. External links are also sometimes found in the indexes for entries linking to other sites.

Links are traditionally created by designating text as hypertext, but links can also be made from graphics, such as navigational "buttons." For text, the default formatting for hypertext is underlined text in blue (changing to purple after the link is visited). If you do nothing special, the text that you designate as a link will appear this way. You can override the default, however, by specifying a different font color. (See previous discussion about the codes for color.) Removing the underlining, though, is more complicated and requires a specification within a "style" of "text-decoration: none." A detailed explanation of HTML styles or "cascading style sheets," however, is beyond the scope of this book.

All three types of links utilize the same HTML tag, the "anchor" tag, indicated by the letter "a." The anchor tag is a container tag, which encapsulates the text to be linkable, or hypertext. It is a tag that contains a descriptive attribute in quotation marks following an equal sign. The descriptive attribute is the destination of the link. The descriptive value follows another code term designating the link destination. This term is "href," which stands for "hypertext reference." The closing container tag that follows the text is </a>. The basic link tag template appears as follows:

```
<a href="link-destination">text to be hypertext</a>
```

Internal Links

For a link within a Web page, also known as a "jump link," the name of the link destination, or "named anchor," is whatever you want to call it. However, you must use a single word followed by a crosshatch or pound sign, #. For example:

```
<a href="#destination">text to be hypertext</a>
```

Creating internal links actually requires a two-part process. In addition to the text coded with the anchor "href" code, which indicates a link to somewhere, you also need to add a code indicating the destination of the link somewhere else on the page. This determines where the browser will jump to when the hyperlinked text is clicked.

The destination is tagged as follows:

```
<a name="destination"></a>
```

Note that the destination named anchor is a pair of container tags that contains nothing. Nothing appears in the browser to indicate the presence of a named anchor.

A common example of an internal link is hypertext at the bottom (or even middle) of a long Web page that says "Top of page." It would be natural, then, to name the anchor "top." For example:

```
<a href="#top">Top of page</a>
```

and at the top of the page, just after the <body> tag, you would have:

```
<a name="top"></a>
```

Internal links are typically used in Web site A–Z indexes to connect letters of the alphabet displayed at the top of the page to the letters of the alphabet used as headings where each alphabetical section of the index actually begins (sometimes called alpha breaks). A–Z indexes tend to have long Web pages, and such jump links eliminate a great deal of scrolling through the index. Another use of internal jumps allows *See* references and *See also* references to work within an index. Thus, clicking on the reference moves to the referred term.

Links Between Pages

Links between pages turn a group of pages into an actual Web site. The home page typically provides links to either all the pages of a site or at least to intermediate pages that then link to all the pages. In turn, all the pages of a Web site ideally have a link back to the home page. Pages within a site may have links between each other. On a Web site A–Z index page, the index entries are linked to other pages of the Web site.

The basic link tag between pages is:

```
<a href="filename.htm">text to be hypertext</a>
```

When you click on the hypertext, the browser opens the named page, starting at the top of the page. The link is to the filename of the file of the page to be linked to, not its title. As mentioned previously, standard HTML pages have names that may end in .htm or .html. Note that some Web sites have pages that have different extensions, such as .php or .asp, which reflect a higher level of programming. But linking to these pages works just the same. HTML file names cannot have spaces in them. Underscores or hyphens are often used for descriptive multi-word filenames.

On a large Web site, pages are often stored within subfolders. If the link occurs between pages within the same subfolder, there is no problem, but if the link occurs between pages in different folders, then the folder of the file to which the link points needs to be included in the link destination, as in the example:

```
<a href="folder/filename.htm">text to be hypertext</a>
```

Instead of hypertext, an image can also act as the link to another page. This often happens with "buttons" that are actually graphics. Here is the code:

```
<a href="siteindex.htm"><img src="siteindex-button.gif"></a>
```

Links to Anchors Within Other Pages

If a named anchor exists within a Web page, you can create a link to it not merely from within the same page, but also from another page. When the user clicks the hypertext on one page, the second page opens at the point where the anchor occurs rather than at the top of the page. This functionally comes from a combination of the internal link and the link-between-pages. The anchor destination specifies the page name with the anchor name immediately following, as in the example:

```
<a href="filename.htm#destination">text to be
hypertext</a>
```

This type of linking is often employed in Web site indexes, whereby an index entry is linked not merely to the top of a page but to a specific section within a page.

External Links

External links perform as connectors to other Web sites. The basic tag template for links between pages is as follows:

```
<a href="website-URL">text to be hypertext</a>
```

Upon clicking the hypertext, the browser opens the named page at the top of the page. URL stands for uniform resource locator and gives the address of the home page of a Web site or of any page within a site, and it is what displays in the address bar of a browser. The URL follows the designator "http://". The designation "http" stands for hypertext transfer protocol. (Occasionally you will see a variation, such as "https://" for hypertext transfer protocol secure.) A specific example is:

```
<a href="http://www.asindexing.org">American Society of
Indexers</a>
```

Sometimes a Web site index will include external links, such as to closely affiliated sites. An A–Z index entirely of external sites is certainly feasible, but less common.

Whether a link functions internally to another page or externally to another Web site, by default the Web browser opens the new page in place of the previous page. The user can return to the previous page with the Back button. For external links, however, it is often preferable to have the Web browser open a new window. This way the Web page of the original Web site remains open and available. It makes users better aware that they are going to an external site. The Back button on the newly opened browser window will not work and will appear grayed out.

To control how the browser opens the new page, you add a descriptive value to the anchor tag. Called the Target, it refers to the target window for the new page. To indicate that the new page should open in a new browser window, use the target="_blank" tag. Note the underscore. So, this is how the link looks:

```
<a href="http://www.asindexing.org" target="_blank">
American Society of Indexers</a>
```

Viewing HTML Code

Once you are familiar with reading HTML code, you will find it instructive to view the code of other Web sites. If using Internet Explorer, select **View** on the menu bar, and in the drop-down menu, select **Source**. A temporary file will open in Notepad, or your default text editor, displaying the source HTML code for the page you were just viewing in the browser. Expand the window to full-screen width so that the text does not wrap so much. If using Netscape, Mozilla, or Firefox, select **View** from the menu bar and, in the drop-down menu, **select Page Source** (control +U). A new browser window will open displaying the source HTML code for the page you were viewing in the browser. Netscape, Mozilla, or Firefox are recommended for viewing because those browsers use colors and bold in View Source, and the tags are easily distinguished from the text.

WEB PAGE EDITING AND UPLOADING
HTML Editing Software

An HTML editor, also known as an authoring tool, is software used to create Web pages in HTML without requiring the user to know and type the HTML tags. Learning the tags from this chapter should be sufficient to create an entire simple Web site using just a text editor. This process, however, can be quite tedious. It is much easier to use an HTML editor when creating or editing a Web site or Web page. Typing or editing the actual HTML code, however, is sometimes preferred when making minor changes. Most HTML editors also provide the option of viewing and editing the code directly.

A wide range of HTML editing software exists. Some programs are free while others cost hundreds of dollars. Below are a number of HTML editors listed by price as of 2006. (Note: WYSIWYG stands for "what you see is what you get" in the user interface.)

- **Mozilla Composer** – Based on Netscape Composer, this is a component of the Mozilla Suite, which includes the Web browser. It features both a WYSIWYG editor and also provides the option of directly editing the HTML coding. Price: Free. Mac and Windows versions. Web site: www.mozilla.org/products/mozilla1.x

- **1st Page 2000** – This is a straight HTML editor (not WYSIWYG). Price: Free. Windows only. Web site: www.evrsoft.com/products.shtml
- **HTML-Kit** – This is a multi-featured HTML editor that includes various preview modes. Plug-ins are available for advanced programming. Price: Free with an option to register for $55 ($49 online). Windows only. Web site: www.chami.com/html-kit
- **PageSpinner** – This is an HTML editor for Macintosh users. It is not completely WYSIWYG, but it does show tagged text in the style that the particular tag would produce. Price: $29.95. Free trial version for 21 days. Mac only. Web site: www.optima-system.com/pagespinner
- **CoffeeCup HTML Editor** – This features both a code editor and a WYSIWYG visual editor. Price: $49.00 (add $34 for FTP program). Free trial version. Windows only. Web site: www.coffeecup.com/html-editor
- **HotDog** – This allows you to type the actual HTML tags while showing you the outcome in another screen. It's not really WYSIWYG, so you need to be sure of how to create the proper tags. Price: $99.95. There is also HotDog PageWiz, designed for beginners. It combines WYSIWYG and text-based editing. Price: $69.95. Free trial version for either product for 15 days. Windows only. Web site: www.sausage.com/hotdog-professional.html
- **Homesite** – This HTML editor comes from the same software developer as the popular professional authoring system Dreamweaver (Macromedia, now owned by Adobe). It includes a WYSIWYG option, or you can tag directly. There are many shortcut buttons as well as the ability to preview your work in a choice of Web browsers. Price: $99.00. Free trial version for 30 days. Windows only. Web site: www.adobe.com/products/homesite
- **NetObjects Fusion MX** – This software is WYSIWYG, but tends to tag a bit better than some other WYSIWYG editors. It also generates site maps so you can see the structure of your site as you build it. Price: $139.95. Free trial version for 30 days. Windows only. Web site: www.netobjects.com/products/html/nfmx.html
- **Microsoft Office FrontPage** – It is known for its WYSIWYG interface, but it also allows you to write the tags directly. It's especially good for converting MS Office documents (Excel worksheets, PowerPoint presentations, Access databases, and Word documents) into Web pages. Price: $199.00. Free trial version for 30 days. Windows only. Web site: www.microsoft.com/products (under office products)
- **Dreamweaver** – This is the most popular HTML editor for professionals. It features both a WYSIWYG editor and the option of directly editing the HTML coding. It also has a Split View to see both code and design views simultaneously. Developed by Macromedia, it is now owned by Adobe.

Price: $399.00. Free trial version for 30 days. Mac and Windows versions. Web site: www.adobe.com/products/dreamweaver
- **Adobe GoLive** – This is a popular HTML editor for professionals (e.g., graphic designers) who use other Adobe products, such as Photoshop and Illustrator. It features both a WYSIWYG editor and also provides the option of directly editing the HTML coding. $399.00. Free trail version for 30 days. Mac and Windows versions. Web site: www.adobe.com/products/golive

Uploading Web Pages

Creating or editing Web pages is not sufficient to create or edit a live Web site. Edited pages need to be uploaded to a Web server on the Internet. You will likely be working under one of the following three situations:

1. Delivering (on disc or by e-mail) edited Web pages to someone else to upload.
2. Working on the internal network of an organization that has its own Web server.
3. Uploading the Web pages from your computer over an Internet connection to the Web server (computer) of a Web hosting service.

If someone else is uploading the files, you have nothing to worry about, and if you are working on an in-house network, instructions for uploading usually are provided. But if you are to upload files from your computer to a Web server, you need:

- Software for uploading files
- The name of the Web hosting server (and possibly subfolder names)
- A login ID and password

If you use a Web hosting service offered through your ISP (Internet Service Provider) or through a service aimed at nontechnical people with personal Web sites, then the Web hosting service will likely offer a method of uploading files to guide you step-by-step through its Web site interface and your Web browser. You will utilize software on the server, and you won't need any additional software on your computer.

The other standard way to upload files from your computer to a host computer on the Internet uses FTP, which stands for "file transfer protocol." It is not any more complicated, and it has the advantage of letting you upload multiple files at once. When you use FTP, you don't work through your Web hosting service's Web site, though. Rather, you employ FTP software that you have acquired to run on your computer. Most HTML editing software packages have an FTP feature built in, so you do not need separate software. But a few HTML editing software packages do not include FTP. This is something to consider when deciding which HTML editing software to use.

FURTHER READING

Castro, Elizabeth. *HTML 4 for the World Wide Web*, 4th Edition. Berkeley, CA: Peachpit Press, 2000.

Freeman, Elisabeth and Eric Freeman. *Head First HTML with CSS & XHTML*. Sebastopol, CA: O'Reilly & Associates, 2005.

Mantaro, Jessica. *FrontPage 2003: The Missing Manual*. Sebastopol, CA: Pogue Press/O'Reilly & Associates, 2005.

McFarland, David. *Dreamweaver 8: The Missing Manual*. Sebastopol, CA: Pogue Press/O'Reilly & Associates, 2005.

Musciano, Chuck and Bill Kennedy. *HTML & XHTML: The Definitive Guide*. Sebastopol, CA: O'Reilly & Associates, 2006.

Niederst, Jennifer. *Web Design in a Nutshell*. Sebastopol, CA: O'Reilly & Associates, 2001.

Tittel, Ed and Natanya Pitts. *HTML 4 for Dummies*, 4th Edition. New York: Wiley Publishing Inc., 2003.

Chapter 3

HTML for Indexes

While the previous chapter provided an overview of HTML codes, this chapter explains in detail the HTML coding behind Web site indexes and how to create a Web site index without Web indexing software. When creating an index in HTML, you have to know how to create the hypertext links and retain the formatting, especially the indented subentries.

HYPERTEXT LINKS IN A–Z INDEXES

A Web site index utilizes two kinds of links—(1) links to other pages in the site for the index entries and (2) internal links (anchors) within the index for jumping from the index entries to different alphabet letter sections. Even when using software tools to automate the process of creating links, it's a good idea to be familiar with the code in case of questions or problems with the links.

Links from Index Entries to Other Pages

An example of the basic link from an index entry to point to the page with the content appears as follows:

```
<a href="contact.html">mailing address</a>
```

In this case, the entry term **mailing address** is linked to the **contact.html** page.

If the page with the content occurs within a subfolder, remember to indicate the folder within the link reference. For example:

```
<a href="resources/devices.html">vendor links</a>
```

In this case, the entry term **vendor links** is linked to the **devices.html** page, which is located within the **resources** folder.

If the index entry is to point to a section within a page, such as under a section heading, you need a named anchor at the section, and the index entry link must indicate the name of the anchor. For example:

```
<a href="profiles.html#board">board of directors</a>
```

In this case, the entry term **board of directors** is linked to the named anchor of **board** within the **profiles.html** page.

Internal Links for Cross-References

Internal links, those consisting of just named anchors, are used within Web site indexes for cross-references (both for *See* and *See also* references). Although a *See* or *See also* reference might instead provide a link directly to the page with content, such a link to another page occurs if there are no subentries. If the referred term has subentries, an internal link to the referred term within the index is more appropriate. For example:

advancement. *See* promotion

which is coded as:

```
advancement. <i>See</i> <a href="#promotion">promotion </a>
```

along with the anchor name in front of the referred term elsewhere within the index:

```
<a name="promotion"></a><a href="staff.htm#promotions">
promotion</a>
```

See also references utilize internal links to the referred term along with the external link to the content, as in the example:

schedule of classes. *See also* class availability

which is coded as:

```
<a href="schedule.html">schedule of classes</a>.
<i>See also</i> <a href="#classav">class availability</a>
```

Internal Links for Letter Navigation

For navigating the index, most Web site indexes have a "ribbon" of the letters of the alphabet, typically at the top of the page, which are each hypertexted to jump to the beginning of a corresponding letter section. For these internal anchor links, the coding might be:

```
<a href="#a"></a>A<a href="#b">B</a> <a href="#c">C</a>
etc.
```

and the letter headings appear below as:

```
<h3><a name="a"></a>A</h3>
```

and further down the page:

```
<h3><a name="b"></a>B</h3>
```

Note that heading tags are often used with the alphabet letters to make them larger than the regular text.

In a similar manner, hypertext "back to top" links may be inserted within an index, at each letter heading or more or less frequently.

HTML CODES FOR SUBENTRY INDENTING

Indenting for subentries presents certain challenges. The tab feature to indent does not exist in HTML. If you use the blockquote tag, it works only for paragraphs separated by blank lines, not for a line directly under another line. The index will then have blank lines between each entry and appear to be double spaced, which is not as easy for the user to skim through. To indent subentries under main entries in an HTML index, without interleaving blank lines, consider choosing from these various other options:

- Multiple spaces
- Definition lists
- Unordered (bulleted) lists
- Style sheets

Which method you select in creating your Web site indexes depends upon (1) what method you are most comfortable with, which may depend on what your indexing software supports, and (2) what the owner of the Web site might want. A summary of which software tools permit which method of subentry formatting and the advantages or disadvantages of the different methods are covered in Chapter 8.

Multiple "Nonbreaking" Spaces

HTML text shows only a single space. In order to insert two or more spaces in a row, you need to use a special character designating a "nonbreaking" space, which is: ** **.

To create a sufficient indent, put about five nonbreaking spaces in a row. The Web indexing tool HTML Indexer will automatically insert nonbreaking spaces, if you choose that option. Here is an example of an indented subentry with multiple nonbreaking spaces:

```
main entry<br>
     <a href="page.htm">
subentry</a><br>
```

Definition Lists

Definition lists are HTML codes for indenting a word or phrase directly under another word or phrase. Definition lists served as the traditional method of creating Web site indexes before the development of Web indexing tools. Although they can be tedious to create by hand-coding, most any HTML editing software should allow you to create definition lists from the software's menu. Definition lists, by default, in HTML editing software generate a single indented line under each main entry. When you have multiple subentries, then you might need to edit the HTML code. The coding of indented subentries with definition list tags is as follows:

```
<dl>
    <dt>main entry one</dt>
        <dd>subentry</dd>
    <dt>main entry two</dt>
        <dd>subentry one</dd>
        <dd>subentry two</dd>
</dl>
```

The Web page text would appear as follows:

main entry one
   subentry
main entry two
   subentry one
   subentry two

Unordered Lists

Unordered lists create indented, bulleted lists of words or phrases. They are somewhat easier to code, whether by hand or with an HTML editor, than are definition lists. The resulting entries have bullets in front of them, which may or may not be desirable for the index style. It is possible to remove the bullets by so indicating within a style sheet.

In this approach, the entire index section, under a given letter of the alphabet, needs to be in an unordered list. What you will create are nested lists. The coding of indented subentries designated by unordered list tags is as follows:

```
<ul>
    <li>main entry one</li>
    <li>main entry two
        <ul>
            <li>subentry one</li>
            <li>subentry two</li>
        </ul>
    </li>
    <li>main entry three</li>
</ul>
```

The Web page text would appear as follows:

    main entry one
    main entry two
        subentry one
        subentry two
    main entry three

It is possible to use only the `<ul>` codes and not the `<li>` codes to achieve indenting without bullets. But you need to hand-code to achieve this and not rely on HTML editing software.

Style Sheets

Finally, indenting instructions can be indicated in the style for a page. You can define different styles in differently named "classes." The styles can be specified within the head portion of the Web page or in a separate file known as a "cascading style sheet" (CSS), which has the extension .css instead of .htm or .html. It is much more common to have the styles defined in a separate style sheet file than in the head portion of the same HTML page. The Web indexing tool HTML Indexer will automatically create styles with a cascading style sheet, if you choose that option. It is not necessary to understand how to create the coding, but since you may encounter it, I will describe it here.

The code for the use of styles uses the definition of "class." This can be incorporated into the paragraph code, as in the following example:

```
<p class="index01">American Society for Information
Science</p>
<p class="index02"><a href="orgpub.shtml">
contact information</a></p>
```

In this case, the class of "index01" indicates main entries, and the class of "index02" is being used for indented subentries. The resulting index excerpt would appear as follows:

> American Society for Information Science
>   contact information

The class can also be incorporated into a division (section) code, as in the following example:

```
<div class="toc">Boston Broadside<br>
<div class=dd>
<a href="/about/boston.shtml#info">about the newsletter
</a><br>
<a href="/resources/broadside.shtml">back issues</a><br>
</div></div>
```

In this case, the class of "toc" is for main entries, and the class of "dd" indicates indented subentries. The resulting index excerpt appears as follows:

> Boston Broadside
>   about the newsletter
>   back issues

USING AN HTML EDITOR TO COMPLETE A WEB INDEX

The type of software called an HTML editor or authoring tool helps create HTML pages without requiring that you personally type in the HTML code. An HTML editor may be used to edit and hyperlink an index created first in a book indexing program (CINDEX, Macrex. SKY, etc.) and then generated as HTML output, or it may be chosen to edit an index copied from and created in a word processor.

If you don't use any indexing software, you'll need to use a word processor as an intermediate step, because HTML editing software cannot alphabetically sort text as a word processor can. When you create the index in a word processor, you should keep the subentries on the same line as main entries, separated by a special character of your choice, such as a vertical bar. This way, the main entries can be alphabetically sorted. After sorting, the code for a line break can replace each vertical bar preceding a subentry.

The basic technique of utilizing an HTML editor to create a Web site index, without Web site indexing software, is explained in the following section. Since there are numerous HTML editors to choose from, menu options are described in only general terms. How to use specific indexing software is explained in the Chapter 4.

Copying Web Page File Names

When creating a link in an HTML editor, it is not necessary to type the complete code, such as `<a name="page.htm">entry</a>`. But it is necessary to type the page file name, such as **page.htm** or **page.htm#anchor**. You can enter this file name into the designated link field in the HTML editor. Prior to creating the link, though, you should create the index entry.

While viewing the Web pages through a Web browser, type the index entries into an indexing program or, if you don't have an indexing program, type them as a list into a word processor. Copy and paste the Web page file names (or file names plus named anchors) into the place of the page locators in indexing programs, or simply next to the corresponding entries if using a word processor.

To obtain the file name (or the file name plus named anchor for the page sections), copy it from the end of the Web page URL (Uniform Resource Locator, or Web address). While viewing the Web page to be indexed in your browser, at the top of the browser window just under the browser menu but above the display of the Web page, you will see a box with the URL of the page. If the Web pages are on your hard drive (which is the preferred method for indexing) and not out on the Web, the URL will appear odd-looking, starting with **file://** instead of **http://** and with a **%20** inserted where there are spaces, such as:

> file:///C:/Documents%20and%20Settings/My%20Documents/
> websites%20to%20index/about.htm

At the very end of the URL, following the last forward slash and ending in .htm or .html, is the file name. In this example it is **about.htm**.

If you are indexing at a heading within the page, check to see if there is already a named anchor at the heading location. In certain cases, the internal links within the page will be obvious, such as when there is a list of hypertext headings near the top of the page that each link to a corresponding heading below. If there are such hypertext headings, you can right-click in your browser on the hypertext and then select **Properties** to obtain the heading's URL link destination including the anchor name. Copy and paste from the URL the file name plus the anchor at the end.

If a hypertext link to the heading is not obvious, then you will need to search for the anchor name within the source code of the Web page. From the browser menu, select **View > Source** or **View > Page Source**. Then search, using **Edit > Find** (**Ctrl+F**) within the source view page for the string: **<a name="**. This will bring you to each anchor. Copy the desired anchor name from between the quotation marks and paste it following a **#** sign that you type following the file name that you have already copied.

Making Page Hyperlinks

Whether you create the index in an indexing program or in a word processor, there is still the step of making index entries hypertext and linked to the appropriate page file name (or file name plus anchor), which is the locator. This involves cutting and pasting each file name (or file name plus anchor).

In your HTML editor, select the locator URL (page file name or file name plus anchor), cut it, and then select the associated main entry or subentry to the left of the locator. Select your HTML editor's Link feature. Then paste (**Ctrl+V**) the URL into the Link location blank. If your index was originally created in an indexing program, the comma preceding each locator may still be there and will need to be deleted. (Some indexing software programs allow you to suppress or delete this comma automatically.) When completed, you should test the links for the page in your browser.

This copying and pasting of file names is the most tedious process of creating a Web site index without a dedicated Web site indexing tool. If your index is not too long, then this task is manageable. For longer jobs, the software is not only cost-effective but will save your sanity!

Indenting Word-Processed Index Entries

An indexing program can save output as HTML that retains indents for the subentries. If, however, a word processor is used instead to create the index, then the indents need to be created in HTML.

After copying and pasting the sorted index into the HTML editor, it is probably most practical to use unordered-list or definition-list formatting to indent the subentries. This must be done line-by-line for each main entry, although multiple subentries might be handled at once depending upon the HTML editor. The special character, such as a vertical bar, that you had typed in front of each subentry in the word processor still needs to be removed, and can be done by Search and Replace.

If the definition lists or unordered lists options in your HTML editor do not work on an existing list (as opposed to selecting the option prior to typing the list entries), then you must use the other option for indenting: type repeated nonbreaking spaces. Add them in your index while it is still in your word processor, prior to copying the index into your HTML editor. If you had inserted a special character, such as a vertical bar, to separate main entries and subentries on the same line in the word processor, then you can use Search and Replace in your word processor to replace the vertical bars with the code for a series of five nonbreaking spaces: **   **. You will also need to replace paragraph line breaks **^p** with HTML linebreaks **
**. This results in an HTML-coded index in your word processor. This can be copied and pasted into the code view of your HTML editor and then further viewed and edited in the WYSIWYG view.

Adding Navigation Letters

The final step in creating a Web site index in an HTML editor involves adding the letters of the alphabet at the top of the page and/or in other locations. If you had created the index in an indexing program, then the individual alphabetical breaks or letter headings will have been automatically placed at the top of each letter section. If you had created the index in a word processor, however, then you will need to type in these letters. Typeset indexes increase the font size of the letters, and you may want to do so here. In HTML, there are no point sizes (unlike word processing), just relative sizes. Select one size larger from the menu or use Heading level 3 or 4.

At each letter heading within the index, insert a named anchor. Place your cursor just before the letter and then insert the named anchor from the menu options. In the box that appears for Anchor Name, just type the letter as the anchor name. Lowercase is fine here. Repeat for each letter heading.

Then the ribbon of navigational letters needs to be added. At the top of your page in the HTML editor, type the letters of the alphabet in one line, placing an extra nonbreaking space between each. Make the letters bigger and/or bold, or use a heading, such as Heading level 3 or 4:

A B C D E F G H I J K L M N O P Q R S T U V W X Y Z

Next, link the navigation letters at the top of the page to the appropriate named anchors below. Do this for each letter, skipping over the letters that have no links. Once linked, your letters will look something like this (with no active links from Q, V, X, or Z):

<u>A</u> <u>B</u> <u>C</u> <u>D</u> <u>E</u> <u>F</u> <u>G</u> <u>H</u> <u>I</u> <u>J</u> <u>K</u> <u>L</u> <u>M</u> <u>N</u> <u>O</u> <u>P</u> Q <u>R</u> <u>S</u> <u>T</u> <u>U</u> V <u>W</u> X <u>Y</u> Z

As a final step, test the letter links in your browser.

WEB INDEXING SOFTWARE

An HTML editor can be considered the most basic tool in creating a Web site A–Z index. It automates the creation of HTML code for links, character style, and the indenting of subentries. But it serves no use in actual indexing or automated linking of entries. Site map creation tools can automatically hyperlink Web page titles to their Web page files, which can act as a basis for creating index entries, but they still do not aid in actual index entry creation. Other software serves both the functions of HTML-creation and indexing.

Software for Web site indexing consists of three kinds:

1. Utilities that help convert a sorted, formatted index into HTML with hypertext links

2. Dedicated, stand-alone software that combines both the term sorting/formatting and hypertext link creation features
3. Indexing features of online help authoring software

Index Conversion Utilities

Index conversion utilities are programs that take an electronic file of an index and convert it to an HTML document with hyperlinked entries. The early freeware programs of WEBIX and INDTOHTM were utilities to convert indexes, already created in different software, into HTML. Copies of WEBIX are still available, but it is rather simple with its command-line interface and text editor for creating the input index file. The Windows version relies on an out-dated DLL VBRUN200.DLL available free from DLL-files.com (www.dll-files.com). The Windows or DOS version can still be obtained from WWWalker Web Development (www.wwwalker.com.au), but no support is available.

Today the most common tool for converting indexes to HTML is HTML/Prep, developed by Leverage Technologies (LevTech). LevTech is also the exclusive authorized agent for North American corporate and government accounts for the indexing program CINDEX. As such, LevTech has developed several software utilities to employ in conjunction with indexes created in CINDEX or other similar indexing programs. HTML/Prep is one of these. It converts a file, with or without Web links as the locators, into an HTML-coded Web page. HTML/Prep is explained in more detail in Chapter 4.

Meanwhile, newer versions of book indexing software, such as CINDEX, SKY, and Macrex, have incorporated some HTML output features. Except for Macrex, though, these features are limited to HTML formatting and do not automatically hyperlink the index entries.

Dedicated, Stand-Alone Web Indexing Software

Two good software options are dedicated to creating Web site indexes by providing the combined capabilities to automatically sort the index, create indented subentries, and capture the target URLs for the hyperlinked entries. One is the commercial software HTML Indexer, which is developed and sold by David M. Brown of Brown Inc. The other is freeware, XRefHT developed by Tim Craven (the developer of WEBIX), available for free downloading from Craven's Web site (publish.uwo.ca/%7Ecraven/freeware.htm). Both these programs exist in Windows versions only. XRefHT is covered in detail in Chapter 5, and HTML Indexer is covered in Chapter 6.

Online Help Indexing Software

Online help authoring tools (also called HAT) aid in creating online documentation (typically help documentation), with its characteristic expandable table of contents links (such as with book icons in Windows), pages that can be read in sequence or by following internal jump links. Online help authoring software has long included the capability to generate alphabetical indexes of topics that are hyperlinked to the relevant page within the help documentation file. The index is designed to work on the documentation texts that are created as part of the help project. Therefore, not only do you have to learn how to use the indexing tool component of the software, but also how the help-authoring software works overall. Although the software is designed to aid in indexing texts that are created within the project rather than existing Web sites, it is possible to import files.

Online help files are traditionally not HTML files, though. But more recently online help for HTML has become common, especially for use over an intranet. Examples of online help tools include RoboHelp and MadCap Flare.

The indexes created in help authoring tools tend to be scrollable and searchable and typically have a type-ahead feature. In Figure 3.1 (created with HTML Help Workshop), I have typed the first four letters of a word "**inde**" and the index jumped to the first entry with these letters. If I add another letter, the index will jump further. There is no need to retype.

While type-ahead and scrolling are attractive features, they take time to load in a Web page. The index itself is not an HTML file, but rather a special file with the extension .hhk that needs to be called up with a java applet program. The delayed time in running the applet and having the index function over the Web makes indexes created with such an online-help tool rather impractical for Web sites. Such indexes are more feasible for intranets, operating over a high-speed network, or for HTML documents stored and accessed on a single desktop computer, such as e-books.

A minor disadvantage with many help-style indexes is that the entries linked to topics are not indicated as such, so they have no underlining. Subentries and main headings without subentries link to the text, but main headings with subentries do not. Additionally, *See also* entries link to their referring entries, but there is no indication of that functionality.

RoboHelp is currently the preferred help authoring tool among professional writers of online help. Some professional indexers also use it for certain clients. It is the tool with the most support, documentation, online discussion, and literature, including information about its indexing features. While other tools might provide comparable indexing features, they are less popular.

FAR HTML is one such little-known help authoring tool. What is interesting about this free software is that its online help, generated in FAR HTML, appears on its Web site at FAR Online Help (helpware.net/FAR/help/hh_start.htm). This includes the index (click on the index tab, since the default is set to the table of contents), a rare example of a scrollable index on the Web. The indexing features are limited and it is a little bit cumbersome to use, especially compared to the professional dedicated indexing tools of CINDEX, Macrex, or SKY. But if you want to create a scrollable index in a frame on every page of a Web site, you have to make some compromises in your indexing tool. With FAR HTML, you don't have to create a help project; you

40 Indexing Specialties: Web Sites

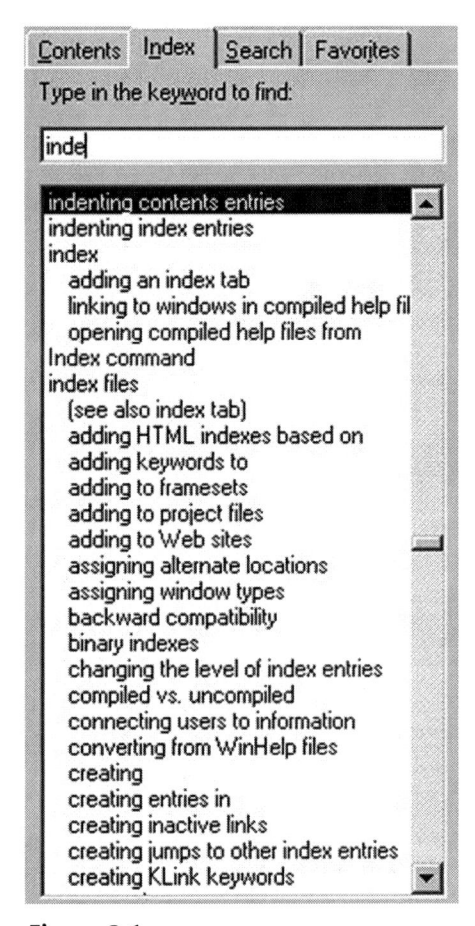

Figure 3.1

can easily index the HTML pages of a Web site and automatically generate the index and table of contents to create a new version of the site in frames, without even having to know how to create frames. FAR HTML acts as a front-end to HTML Help Workshop, which can also be downloaded for free.

Using an online help authoring tool purely for its indexing feature is probably not practical, especially for the more expensive tools. Online help authoring tools are designed not to index general Web sites, but rather HTML documents kept on a single computer or on an intranet. Freelance Web site indexers prefer not to use an online help authoring tool. If, however, you are required to create a scrollable help-style index, then an online-help authoring tool presents a good choice. Since software users have become accustomed to these scrollable searchable indexes within their online help documentation, some Web developers are likely to look for this type of index for a growing number of HTML documents, beyond traditional help documentation. Therefore, you may want to familiarize yourself with at least the free HTML Help Workshop and FAR HTML in case a future project calls for it.

FURTHER READING

Holcomb, Kelley. "Using FAR to Index HTML Help Projects." (6-page PDF file) helpware.net/FAR/bmc_far_Indexing_tutorial.pdf

Rowland, Marilyn Joyce. "Web Site Indexing." Prepared for the Web Indexing Workshop, presented at the June 1999 Annual Conference of the American Society of Indexers and updated July 2000. www.web-indexing.org/resources-rowland-webindexing.htm

SOFTWARE RESOURCES

Help authoring tools that create HTML-based online-help and indexes for the online-help:

AuthorIT, in enterprise and workgroup editions at variable pricing, www.author-it.com

Doc-to-Help for Word, $749.95, Doc-to-Help Enterprises, $999.95, www.doctohelp.com

FAR HTML shareware, helpware.net/FAR/

HDK (Hypertext Development Kit) from Virtual Media RepubliCorp, $549, www.vmtech.com/hdk.htm

HyperText Studio from Olson Software, Professional Edition, $349, www.olsonsoft.com

MadCap Flare, $899, www.madcapsoftware.com/products/flare

RoboHelp 6 from Adobe, $999, www.adobe.com/products/robohelp

WebWorks ePublisher Express from Quadralay Corp., $995, www.webworks.com

Chapter 4

Book Indexing Software for Creating Web Indexes

The most efficient way to create a back-of-the-book index is to use dedicated book indexing software, such as CINDEX, Macrex, or SKY Index Professional. (I will refer to these dedicated packages as book indexing software throughout this chapter.) The Web indexing tools currently available do not compare in their functionality and features for manipulating index entries. Therefore, if you already own one of these book indexing software packages (which may cost up to $535 for a single user license), outputting an index created in this software into an HTML index may be the best approach for you. You already know the program, so you are much more likely to produce better indexing with it. If the same index will appear in both print and Web formats, you will find this the most efficient approach.

The latest versions of the most popular book indexing programs of CINDEX, Macrex, and SKY Index all provide options to generate the index as HTML output. The output created this way, however, is not necessarily the final product meant to serve as a functional hyperlinked Web site index. More editing may be required depending upon each program's capability. It is important to distinguish an index generated as an HTML file from an HTML index that links to the actual Web text.

To link the index to the text involves embedding the appropriate hyperlink within each index entry. This includes the HTML coding for a hyperlink (<a href="URL">text</a>) and the specific URL for each link. Here and in the following chapters, I use the term "URL" to refer to the Web site index locator—consisting of the Web page file name, possibly with the addition of the named anchor, and possibly with the addition of a file folder—even though it is only part of the complete Web page URL.

It is your decision where to input the URL in your book indexing program: in the page locator field, in a subentry field, or even in the main entry field when there are no subentries. You may also choose whether to enter just the URL and later edit the HTML generated index in your HTML editing software to create the hyperlinks, or whether to enter the hyperlink coding, too, within your book indexing program's entries. If you do not wish to enter the hyperlink coding, I recommend entering the URL in the page locator field and taking care of the hyperlinking later. If you choose to enter the hyperlink coding, then I recommend entering it, along with the URL, in a subentry field. If you input the hyperlinked coding and URL in the page field, hypertext will appear on screen next to the main entry. This may confuse users, but you still might choose to do this, especially if you linked to page numbers. If you enter the hyperlinked coding and URL in the subentry field, the hypertext will be indented under the main entry. This approach makes sense and looks cleaner, especially if you have one or more subentries. If you place the hyperlinked coding and URL in the main entry field, the main entry will become hypertext as desired, but your indexing program will not properly sort and group main entries due to interference from the HTML coding. Thus, each option has its disadvantages.

As for entering the hyperlink within the index entries, you do not necessarily have to type out the coding, depending upon your software. If you use CINDEX, you can run an additional utility program called Mapper that saves you the tedium of typing the code. If you use SKY Index, you can create a macro or use the program's translation table feature for the same purpose. If you use Macrex, the program's HTML index feature has the hyperlink coding built in. Finally, if you use another program to convert any index to a Web index, such as HTML/Prep or XRefHT, then you avoid typing any of the hyperlinking code yourself, since the software will automatically generate the code.

The first part of this chapter covers the procedures to create HTML output and the steps needed to edit that output into a fully functional Web index for each of the major commercial book indexing programs. The second part of this chapter examines the utility program HTML/Prep and the conversion feature of XRefHT to automate some of the steps in converting a book index into a fully hyperlinked Web index. When using HTML/Prep or XRefHT's conversion feature, you will enter the URL in the book indexing program's page locator field; you do not need to type in the hyperlink coding.

Be aware that if the URL contains numerals within it and you enter it in the page locator field, depending on the book indexing program, the software might interpret the numerals as page numbers and alter them, such as removing leading zeros. If you notice such problems with locators, either temporarily substitute a different special character by means of Search and Replace throughout the text, or use the map/translation table feature of your book indexing software (the translation table in SKY Index, or the character replacement table in the Macrex Word Processor [.mwp] settings). With CINDEX and other Windows programs, you can use the utility Mapper, described later, or the Windows Character Map table (Start > Programs > Accessories > System Tools > Character Map) for this purpose.

CINDEX-CREATED INDEXES

CINDEX software is sold and supported by Indexing Research of Rochester, New York. Of the three major dedicated indexing programs, creating HTML output from CINDEX requires the greatest amount of editing. On the other hand, the corporate distributor of CINDEX, Leverage Technologies Inc., offers various utility programs to help create HTML output that work especially well with CINDEX. In CINDEX, to save the index as HTML output, the option of **HTML Tagged Text** can be selected from the **Save as** options. These tags, by themselves and left unchanged, are not sufficient for creating a properly formatted HTML Index. You either need to create a CSS style to which the tags may refer, or you need to modify the tags, as described here.

When inputting index entries in CINDEX, enter the main heading and subentries as usual, but in the page field or the lowest subentry field, put the Web URL in the place of page numbers. In Figure 4.1, the main heading is **pay schedules,** and the locator is **hr/payroll.htm#schedule.**

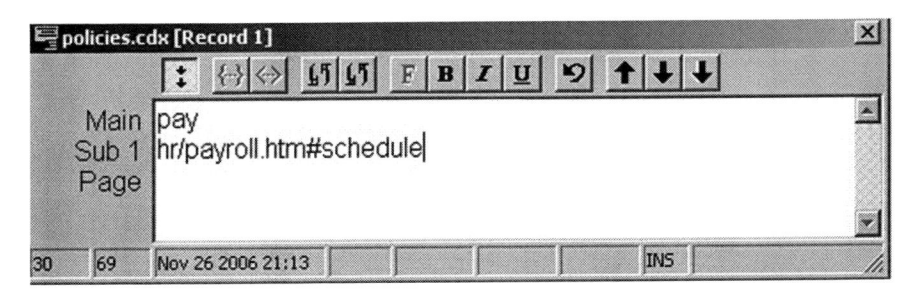

Figure 4.1

Entering the URL as such will necessitate editing the generated index in your HTML editing program or using a conversion program (HTML/Prep or XRefHT) afterward in order to make the main entry actually hyperlinked to the URL. If you were to type the additional HTML code for the hyperlink into the index entry, it will remain as code when the index is generated as HTML. The HTML output from CINDEX takes care of the formatting but does not include translations of links.

There is a software utility called Mapper that can help automate the process of inputting the URL in the index entries. Available for $125 (2006 price) from Leverage Technologies, Inc., Mapper utilizes a map file that you create in order to convert page fields from one reference to another. It is, thus, ideal for the process of replacing or augmenting page locators with URLs. You can call on Leverage Technologies' technical support to help with creating the map file if you experience difficulty. For larger and more complicated projects, Leverage Technologies also creates custom applications that serve specifically to transform print locators into hyperlinks.

Note that for Web page names that contain a hyphen, you need to change your default CINDEX settings. If you leave it as the default, when you enter the page

46   Indexing Specialties: Web Sites

locator field, CINDEX will change the hyphen to an "en" dash. To prevent this from happening, in CINDEX select from the pull-down menu **Documents > Page References**, and in the section for **Page Ranges**, for **Connecting Text**, replace the dash (the default setting) with a hyphen.

When you are finished indexing, save the index as HTML Tagged Text (.tag) by selecting **Save as type** from the drop-down list shown in Figure 4.2.

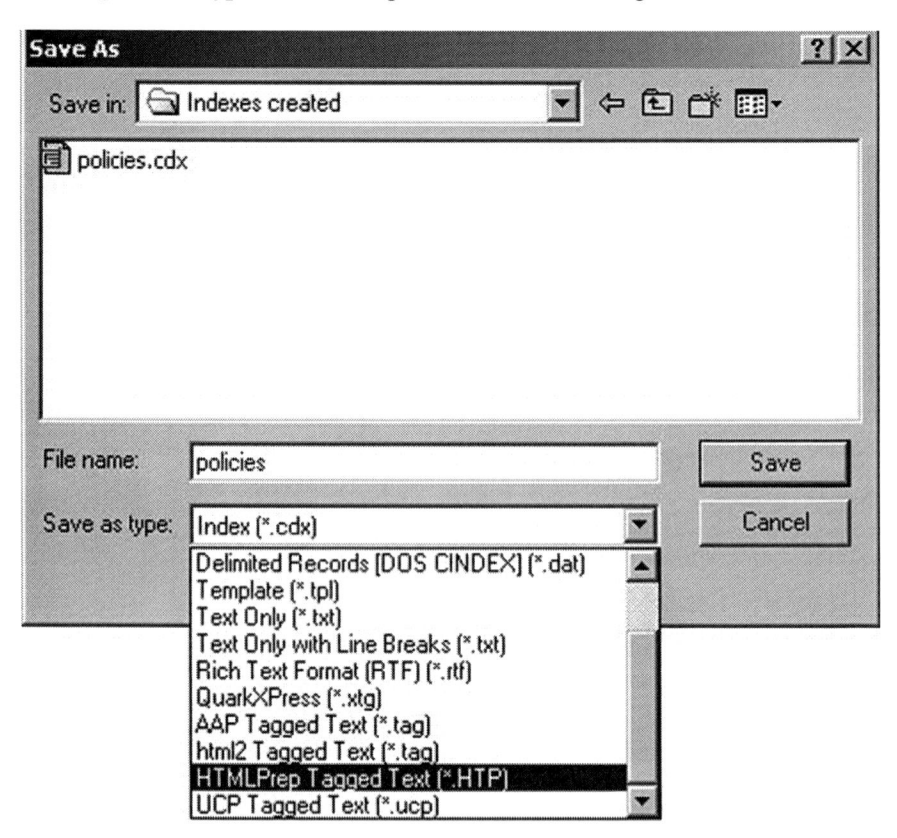

Figure 4.2

In HTML Tagged Text, the default tags for the main heading and subentry levels are HTML heading tags, such as <h1> for the main heading and <h2> for the subentry. These might seem inappropriate for a standard index style, but in fact, they can be used if your index Web page defines the heading tags in a way appropriate for an index. You do this by writing CSS style, which you insert in the nondisplayed Head portion of the HTML index or on a separate style sheet page. An example of how to write the style appears at the end of this chapter in the section "XRefHT for Converting Indexes."

If writing an HTML style seems too complicated, then take another approach by simply changing the HTML tags in CINDEX. You can change the default tags by selecting the HTML tag set from the main menu. Select **Tools > Markup tags...** and then **HTML.ctg** from the dropdown list of Tag sets. You may either select **Edit** to permanently change the tags, or select **Duplicate** to retain the existing version and create a new tag set based on it. If you select Duplicate, then you must give the duplicate tag set a new name of your choice (minus the extension).

In either case, delete the heading tags for the levels of entries and replace them with tags for indenting subentries, repeated nonbreaking spaces, which is ** ** and with tags for line breaks **
, following the template shown in the screenshot in Figure 4.3. Insert twice as many nonbreaking spaces for Level 3 as for Level 2 in order to further indent sub-subentries. Then click on **OK.

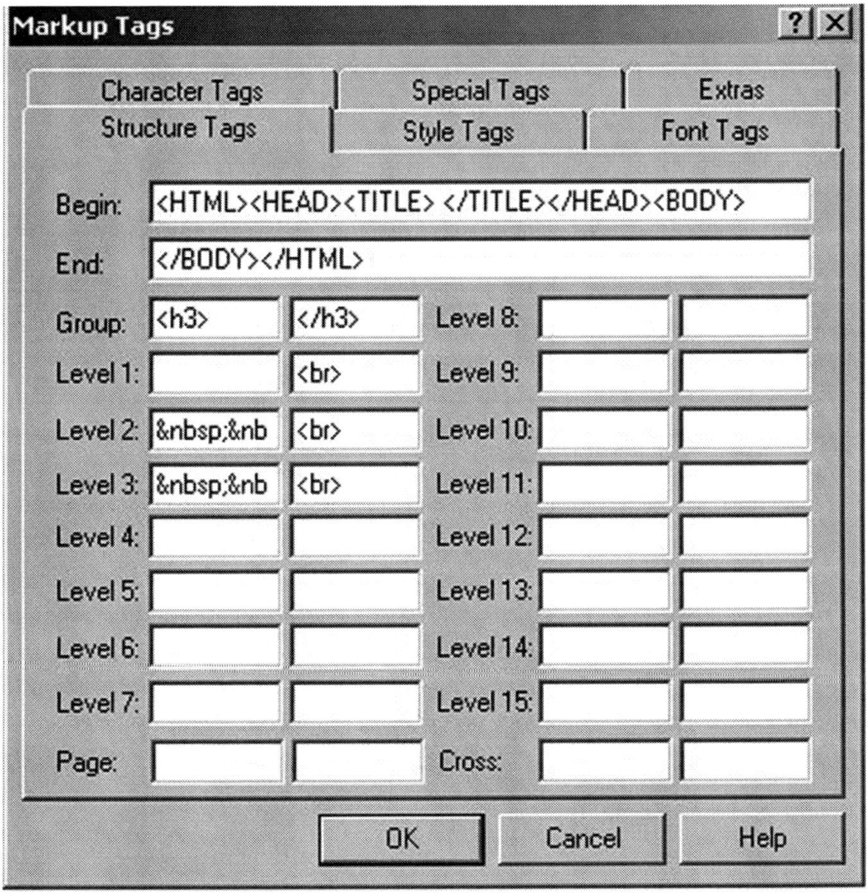

Figure 4.3

If you choose to create a new tag set based on a **Duplicate**, when you select **File > Save As...**, under **Save as type**, you will now see the name of the new file type that you created.

When you save your index, under **File > Save As...**, select the edited HTML.ctg or the newly named duplicate tag set you have created. After you save the index, you will have to change the file name in your operating system's file manager so that the file will have the extension of either **.html** or **.htm**. Only then is it a valid HTML page that you may open and view in a browser.

When you view the index in your Web browser, it will need more editing work. It is a valid HTML page, and the subentries are appropriately indented, but the index entries lack hyperlinking, and the navigational letters of the alphabet need formatting. Another minor detail to note in CINDEX-created HTML indexes has to do with the presentation of letters of the alphabet. The letter falls on the same line as the first entry of the letter group so you must move it. You must take care of all of these changes using your HTML editing program.

Editing the CINDEX-Generated Web Page Index

When you open the CINDEX-created index file in your HTML editing program, you will notice that the heading letters of the alphabet lie on the same line as the first main entry that follows it, as in the example that follows (where URLs were entered into the Page field without hyperlinking code):

> A address of the library, contact.htm
> art exhibits, art.htm
>   current exhibit, art.htm#current
>   past exhibits, art_past.htm
> author events, guest_speakers.htm
>
> B blog for readers' reviews, help_readers_reviews.htm
> Board of Trustees, trustees-endowment.htm

You must manually add line breaks and an extra blank line after each letter.

If you had entered only URLs without any hyperlinked coding (`<a href="URL">`, `</a>`), then you still have to convert the individual locators into hyperlinks. As explained in the previous chapter, to do this, you will need to move (cut) each locator URL from its position adjacent to the main entry or subentry and make it the target of a hypertext link. This involves repeated cutting and pasting:

1. Select the URL and cut it (**ctrl +X**).
2. Highlight main entry or subentry text associated with the URL to its left.
3. In your HTML editor's menu, select the Link function. (This will vary depending upon your program.)

4. Paste (**ctrl+V**) the URL into the Link location blank to create an internal link. The index entry should then be hyperlinked to the URL.

After hyperlinking all the entries, remove any commas preceding each locator by performing a global Search and Replace.

The final step to create a Web site index in an HTML editor requires adding in the letters of the hypertext alphabet at the top of the page and/or in additional locations. Then hyperlink them to the corresponding letters within the index. See the previous chapter for details on how to do this.

SKY INDEX-CREATED INDEXES

SKY Index Professional is sold and supported by SKY Software of Stephens City, Virginia. In SKY Index, to save the index as HTML output, a preset HTML output is available for selecting among the list of Output Formats. Unlike in CINDEX, you neither need to create a style nor change the HTML tagging.

You may enter the URL in the Page locator field, in a Subentry field, or even in the Main entry field when there are no subentries. In the screenshot in Figure 4.4, the main entry is **pay schedules,** and the locator, **hr/payroll.htm#schedule**, has been added to the Page field.

Main	Sub1	Page
pay schedules		hr/payroll.htm#schedule

Figure 4.4

Entering the simple URL as shown in Figure 4.4 will necessitate editing the generated index or using a conversion program (HTML/Prep or XRefHT) afterward to make the main entry actually hyperlinked to the URL.

Alternatively, you can enter the complete hyperlinking code, such as **\<a href="hr/payroll.htm#schedule"\>** pay schedules\</a\>, in either the Main, Sub1 (or lower level Sub2 or Sub3, etc.) or Page fields. SKY Index's HTML output feature recognizes the hyperlinking code and converts it to a functional link. In the screenshot in Figure 4.5, the term is broken into a main entry and subentry, with the subentry coded for hyperlinking.

Main	Sub1	Page
pay	\<a href="hr/payroll.htm#schedule"\>schedules\</a\>	

Figure 4.5

To facilitate the entry of the code, you can use SKY Index's translation table feature. To open the translation table, go to **Options > Data Entry Options >**

50 Indexing Specialties: Web Sites

Translations. You can designate one special character or an abbreviation for `<a href="`, another one for: `">`, and a third for `</a>`. You can also designate a special character or an abbreviation for a commonly typed URL.

You may also choose to use an additional level of subentries just for the hyperlinking. SKY Software has even created a small free utility program to aid in this procedure. You enter the URL in the Page field, as you normally would, but through a single export and import, you can promote the page locator contents to the lowest level of subentry. The utility can be downloaded from the SKY Software Web site.

Note that if you are indexing a Web page name that has a hyphen within it and you enter it in the page locator field, SKY Index will change the hyphen to an "en" dash. To prevent this from happening, in SKY Index, select from the pull-down menu **Options > Index Options > Locators**, and under **Page Runs**, select **Dash**.

Furthermore, to prevent a comma from being generated between the index entry and locator, which is the default book indexing style, go to **Options > Index Options > Locators**, and delete the comma that is the **Leader** for **Locators**.

At any point during the entry creation process prior to generating the index, select from the menu **Options > Index Options**. Then select the bottom-most tab for **Output Format**. Under **Presets**, select **HTML**. You will then notice various values that have automatically been filled in, as appears in the screenshot in Figure 4.6. Click **OK**.

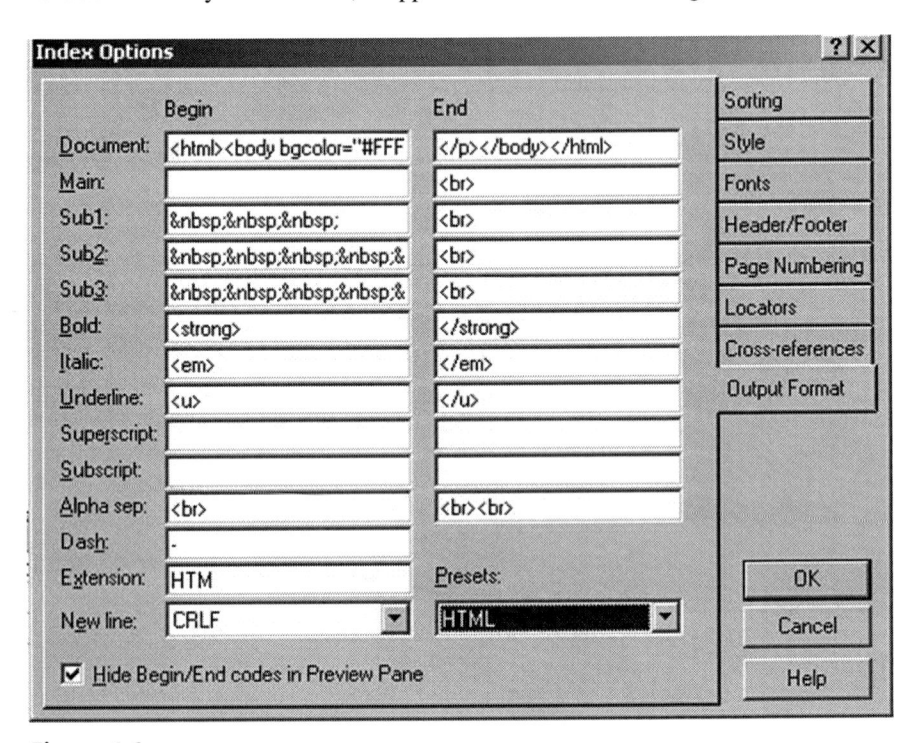

Figure 4.6

You may then generate the index as usual: **Index > Generate**.

Editing the SKY Index-Generated Web Page Index

In your HTML editor, open the index file, which now has the extension .htm. You will notice that not only are subentries appropriately indented, but any cross-references also have internal jump links.

If you had entered only URLs without any hyperlinked coding (<a href="URL">, </a>), then you still have to turn the individual locators into hyperlinks. To do this, you will need to move each locator URL from its position adjacent to the main entry or subentry and make it the destination of the link. Select the URL, cut it (**ctrl +X**), and then highlight the main entry or subentry associated with it to the left. In your HTML editor's menu, select the Link function. (This will vary depending upon your program.) Then paste (**ctrl+V**) the URL into the Link location blank to create an internal link. The index entry should then be hyperlinked to the URL.

The final step in creating a Web site index, which is done in an HTML editor, is adding in the letters of the hypertext alphabet at the top of the page and/or in additional locations and hyperlink them to the corresponding letters within the index. The steps for doing this are provided in the previous chapter.

MACREX-CREATED INDEXES

Macrex is sold by Macrex Indexing Services in the United Kingdom, and is also sold and supported by the North American Macrex Support Office headed by Gale Rhoades in Daly City, California. The procedure for creating HTML indexes in Macrex is a little more complicated than with CINDEX or SKY Index, but the capabilities and options are far greater. In fact, Macrex can take care of most of the steps, and you may not even need to use HTML editing software to complete the task and format the index. Most significantly, the software automatically creates hypertext entries, linking to the appropriate place in the files being indexed, either to the appropriate page or to an anchor within the Web page. You can either make the last subentry the link or have the final index entries point to multiple targets. Instead of having to actually type a "locator," you can use the autonumbering feature of Macrex in combination with copying and pasting.

The options for creating an HTML index are found under the **Options Menu** (option 7): **Hypertext markup features**. The default hypertext markup features that display are shown in the screenshot in Figure 4.7.

Before you proceed, however, you need to load a markup file, as the menu suggests. In fact, there are a total of seven definition files that are required for the successful creation and display of an HTML index. Depending on the version of Macrex you purchased, you may or may not have all these definition files already. If you don't have them, you can obtain them free of charge along with instructions and e-mail support from your Macrex representative. Since the procedure is rather

52 Indexing Specialties: Web Sites

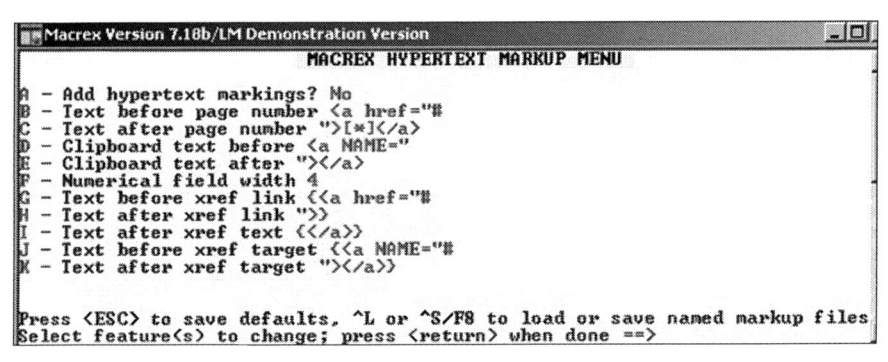

```
Macrex Version 7.18b/LM Demonstration Version
                    MACREX HYPERTEXT MARKUP MENU
A - Add hypertext markings? No
B - Text before page number  <a href="#
C - Text after page number   ">[*]</a>
D - Clipboard text before    <a NAME="
E - Clipboard text after     "></a>
F - Numerical field width 4
G - Text before xref link    <<a href="#
H - Text after xref link     ">>
I - Text after xref text     <</a>>
J - Text before xref target  <<a NAME="#
K - Text after xref target   "></a>>

Press <ESC> to save defaults, ^L or ^S/F8 to load or save named markup files
Select feature(s) to change; press <return> when done ==>
```

Figure 4.7

involved, I will not go into the details here, but the Macrex Support Office can provide step-by-step guidance for Macrex users.

In addition to automatically hyperlinking the entries to the locator URLs, Macrex also inserts the hypertext letters of the alphabet at the top of the page and/or in additional locations. Cross-references also receive hypertext links.

HTML/PREP FOR CONVERTING INDEXES

As we have seen, the HTML output from dedicated book indexing programs can require considerable editing, especially if you enter in only the URL and not any hyperlinking code. This is where a conversion utility becomes useful. Among the kinds of software available for Web site indexing are utility programs that help convert a sorted, formatted index into HTML with hypertext links.

The only commercial utility program for this purpose is HTML/Prep. The shareware XRefHT also has this feature. The index entries and subentries, however, need to be created first, and this is typically done in a back-of-the-book indexing program, such as CINDEX or SKY Index. (Macrex indexes do not require conversion.) Prior to conversion, the index does not even have to be in HTML. Thus, indexes created in other programs, such as wINDEX, that do not have an HTML output feature, may also be converted to Web indexes by using HTML/Prep or XRefHT.

HTML/Prep is a Windows command-line application for converting a tagged index into an HTML file with functioning links. It is available from its developer Leverage Technologies in Cleveland, Ohio, and, as of the time of writing this book, its price is $125. Unfortunately, there is no free demo version. However, there are links to several indexes created using HTML/Prep from its Web page.

HTML/Prep automatically does the following to your index:

- Indents subentries

- Makes the entries hyperlinked to the Web page file name that you have entered in the page field
- Adds hyperlinked letters for navigation at either the top of the page, at top and bottom, or in a separate page/file, linked to letter headings within the index
- Makes cross-references hyperlinked
- Includes various formatting options

Preparing an Index for HTML/Prep Conversion

When creating an index to be converted in HTML/Prep, enter simple URLs (without additional coding) into the field for page locators. In fact, you don't even need to type in the full file name. You may leave off the extension .htm or .html and let HTML/Prep automatically add it. The URLs must be entered in the locator field, though, and not in a subentry field.

When you are finished indexing, you must save the index file with specialized tags, not HTML tags, which provide instructions to HTML/Prep on where to apply various conversions. Some indexing software tools, such as CINDEX or SKY Index, provide tag set templates, which you may use or modify. For indexes created in other programs, including word processors, you must add the HTML/Prep tags manually to the generated index by means of some clever Search and Replace. As such, HTML/Prep can be used on indexes created in any method.

An index written as follows:

> A
> address of the library, contact.htm
> activities, children's, programs.htm <I>, see also</I> events
> art exhibits, art.htm
>   current exhibit, art.htm#current
>   past exhibits, art_past.htm
> author events, guest_speakers.htm

should be tagged as follows:

> <g>A
> <l0>address of the library <c> contact.htm
> <l0>activities, children's <c> programs.htm <x><I>, see also</I> events
> <l0>art exhibits <c> art.htm
> <l1>current exhibit <c> art.htm#current
> <l1>past exhibits <c> art_past.htm
> <l0>author events <c> guest_speakers.htm

(That is a lowercase letter "l" for the heading levels.) The complete set of HTML/Prep tags is listed in the documentation that accompanies the software.

Preparing a CINDEX-Created Index for HTML/Prep

HTML/Prep is easiest to use with CINDEX. The HTML/Prep package comes with a style sheet and HTML/Prep tag set for CINDEX (although you don't have to understand how these work). Before the first execution of HTML/Prep, you must issue a command in HTML/Prep indicating the version of CINDEX you are using, which causes the style sheet and tag set to be saved where CINDEX will find them.

As you index, insert the URLs in the Page field in CINDEX. Remember that for Web page names that contain a hyphen, you need to change your default CINDEX settings so that hyphens are not changed to "en" dashes. In CINDEX, select from the pull-down menu **Documents > Page References**, and in the section for **Page Ranges**, for **Connecting Text**, replace the dash (the default setting) with a hyphen.

After completing the index in CINDEX, simply select from the menu **File > Save As**. Then in the **Save as type** drop-down list, scroll down and select **HTMLPrep Tagged Text (*.HTP)**. Next, run HTML/Prep on this tagged text file.

Preparing a SKY Index-Created Index for HTML/Prep

For SKY Index-created indexes, before generating the index to convert with HTML/Prep, you need to set the correct output format tags. This is not one of the Preset choices, but rather you need to create a custom set of tags. From the main menu, select **Options > Index Options**, and the select the bottom-most tag for **Output Format**. In the scroll box for **Presets**, scroll down and select the last choice **<Custom>**. (Even though the end result will be HTML, do *not* select the Preset for HTML.) Now you need to fill in the blanks as in the example shown in Figure 4.8. These tags are also listed in the HTML/Prep documentation.

Then generate the index. The generated index will have the same file name but now the extension .txt. Next, run HTML/Prep on this tagged text file.

Running HTML/Prep

HTML/Prep is a command-line utility, and as such, it has no interface of its own. You merely invoke the program at a command-line prompt. If you are not familiar with command-line mode operations, this might seem intimidating, but it is actually quite easy to do. As an alternative, Leverage Technologies also offers a free utility called WinCommand, which lets you create an icon to run HTML/Prep from the Windows desktop or a folder. You can then type into the WinCommand dialog box instead of at the command-line prompt. Nevertheless, you will need to read the HTML/Prep documentation thoroughly, since there are no intuitive menus.

In Windows, the Command Prompt is available in the Accessories folder, within the Programs folder (where Notepad is also located). Once launched, the first thing to do is change the directory (folder) by typing the command of **cd** followed by the

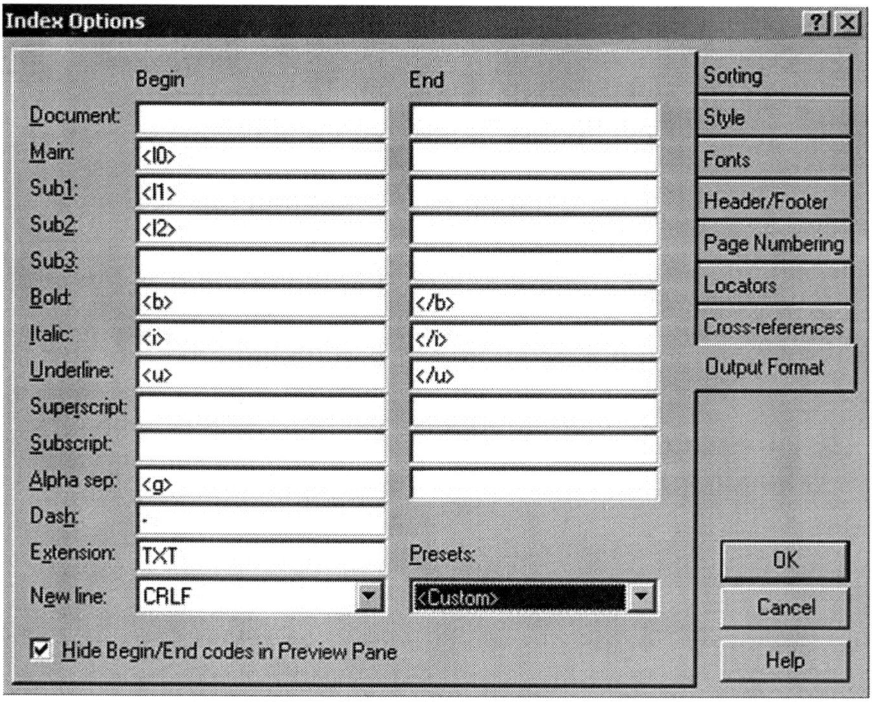

Book Indexing Software for Creating Web Indexes 55

Figure 4.8

folder path where HTML/Prep is located. In the example shown in Figure 4.9, the folder is called C:\Program Files\Leverage Technologies\htmlprep.

After changing to the appropriate directory/folder, type the command **htmlprep**, followed by the index file name without any extension, in this case **test**, and followed by any additional options. In the example shown in Figure 4.9, I have selected the options of **–lh**, which is to display the lowest heading as the link text and use the locator as the link value (as opposed to the default hypertext phrase "Click here"), and **–lt**, which is to place the letter list only at the top of the output file (as opposed to the default placement in a separate file). Thus, I have typed the following command:

```
htmlprep test -lh -lt
```

The program then shows that it has processed the index, indicating the number of lines and headings. (This was a very short one.) An index file with the same name, but now with the extension .htm will have been created in the same folder. In this case it is called test.htm. No further editing in an HTML editor is needed.

56 Indexing Specialties: Web Sites

```
C:\>cd Program Files\Leverage Technologies\htmlprep

C:\Program Files\Leverage Technologies\htmlprep>htmlprep test -lh -lt

HTML/Prep(tm), Copyright 1995-2007 Leverage Technologies, Inc. All righ
ed.
>> Determining group breaks and main heading anchors ...
    45 lines scanned
    12 group breaks prepared (12 with entries)
>> Processing index (test.htp) ...
    45 index lines input
   204 lines output
    19 main headings output
     2 main head/xr nonmatches
```

Figure 4.9

XREFHT FOR CONVERTING INDEXES

Although the software XRefHT is best known as a dedicated Web site indexing program, it also includes a feature to convert an index created in dedicated book indexing software or a word processor. This is indeed a useful method if the index has to appear in both print and online forms. Before converting the index, which must be a text file with the suffix .txt, it should have subentries (and any sub-subentries) indented by tabs or double spaces, and it should have a special character preceding the URL locator. If preparing the index in book indexing software, type the URLs (without additional coding) in the page field.

To designate a special character prior to the URL for a CINDEX-created index, such as a vertical bar, in CINDEX go to **Document > Page References**. Then for **Punctuation**, replace the comma with the vertical bar | or other special character. Then save the index as text output, rather than the usual RTF. To do this, select **File > Save as** from the main menu. Then, from the dropdown box **Save as Type**, select either **Text Only** or **Text Only with Line Breaks**. Making note of the file name and location, click on **Save**. Open this text file in XRefHT.

To designate a special character prior to the URL for a SKY Index-created index, such as a vertical bar, in SKY Index go to **Options > Index Options** and then select **Locators.** Then under **Locators, Leader**, replace the comma with the | or other special character. Then save the index as text output, rather than the usual RTF. A preset text output is available for selecting among the list of Output Formats. At any point during the indexing, select from the menu **Options > Index Options**. Then select the bottom-most tab for **Output Format**. Under **Presets**, select **Text (ASCII)**. Click on **OK**. Then generate the index as usual: **Index > Generate**. You will then open this file in XRefHT.

When using XRefHT to convert an index, open the program but do not enter anything into the Heading, Subheading, or URL fields. Under the **File** menu, select **Convert text file > Index…**; do *not* use **Indented**. Browse and open the file of the index that you have saved as text. Click on **Open**. You will then be prompted for the name of the HTML output file. After supplying a name, click on **Save**. A **Convert text file index** dialog box will appear as shown in Figure 4.10.

For **Head levels**, it is recommended to select 6, which is the maximum number in HTML standards, even if you will not have that many levels. This ensures that all browsers will properly read the page. For **URL tag**, insert the special character you had designed when saving your index, such as the vertical bar.

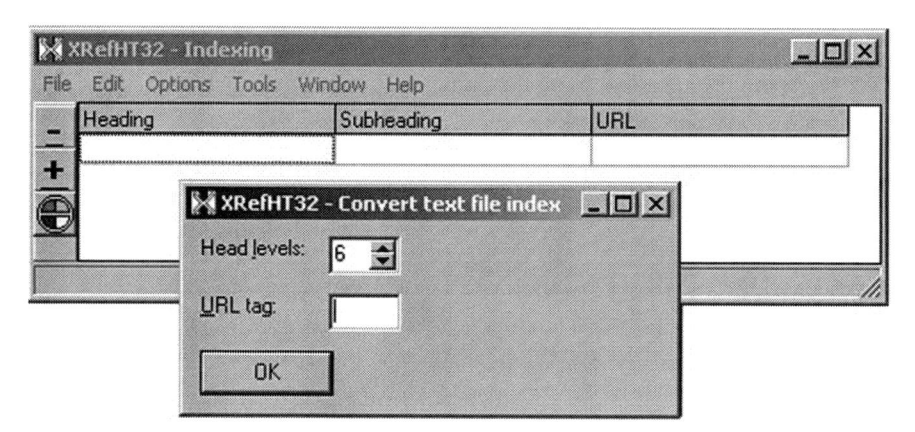

Figure 4.10

As a result, the H1 heading tags will be used for the letter separators and the main entries, H2 tags for the subentries, H3 tags for the sub-subentries, and so on. Of course, you will not want an index displayed this way. So you will have to designate that the headings be used for a different style, other than large and bold, but instead standard small size and indented. You can do this by inserting the following style code within the Head section of your Web index:

```
<head>
<title>Index</title>
<style>
H1, H2, H3, H4, H5, H6 {font-family: Arial, Helvetica,
sans-serif; text-align: left; font-weight: normal; font-
size: smaller; line-height: 0.1}
H2 { text-indent: 2em}
H3 { text-indent: 4em}
H4 { text-indent: 6em}
H5 { text-indent: 8em}
H6 { text-indent: 10em}
</style>
</head>
```

Use the code view of your HTML editor to insert the code. If you cannot figure out how to do it, you can simply convert the index using 0 Head levels, in which case a bulleted list with bulleted indentations for subentries will be created. You will have to edit it, because the letter separators will also be bulleted.

A hypertext index entry can link to only one location, whereas a printed index entry often has multiple page number locators. HTML/Prep can create hyperlinks from page numbers instead of the index entry, if you choose, but XRefHT does not provide this option; only the text itself is hyperlinked. If an index is intended for both print and Web, then slightly different versions need to be created for each. A good strategy is to index with single locators first, as required for the Web index, generate the Web index, and then edit the index entries to gather together locators for the printed index version. Techniques for indexing a single concept found on multiple Web pages are discussed in Chapter 8.

CONVERTING PRINTED INDEXES TO HTML

This chapter has focused on how to create Web site or HTML indexes using dedicated book indexing software, with or without additional conversion programs. To create an index to exist in both printed and Web site versions involves additional considerations. You cannot convert page ranges into URLs, and you cannot have multiple undifferentiated hyperlinked locators. You might also want to link to a more specific (i.e., paragraph) level. So, in practical terms, if you know from the start of a project that the index will be published both in print and online, you might want to create index entries first to the more specific of the two versions, which is the Web site version. After saving that index project, you then edit the index project (still in your book indexing software) so it satisfies printed index style standards. Thus, you are not really "converting a book index to HTML" but rather the opposite: You are converting a Web index to book format. On the other hand, if an existing book index is later to be published on a Web site, you will have to make some sacrifices in usability and style. For example, you will probably create hyperlinked page numbers, rather than hyperlinked entries, and have a series of individually hyperlinked page numbers following an entry. For page ranges, you could indicate the first followed by a plus sign. In the following example, the underlined numbers are hyperlinked:

Pension program, 12, 34+, 57

Since there are no standards, you might like to experiment to see what works best and what the publisher likes. Consider using your software's translation table or the utility Mapper to convert print page locators to URLs.

You could, of course, simply publish a book index as an HTML page on a Web site without actually hyperlinking the entries to the text. This is what is meant by a "Web-mounted index." The major book indexing programs all support this simple HTML output of an index and may even include the additional feature of hyperlinking cross-references and navigational heading letters of the alphabet. A publisher may desire such an HTML output to put the index on a Web site, such as for promotional purposes to let prospective buyers browse it. In other cases, a simple PDF conversion of the index may be deemed acceptable for a Web site posting of the index.

In conclusion, whatever tool(s) you use should depend on what you already own. If you already own a dedicated book indexing program, use what you have. If you do not own dedicated book indexing program but are considering purchasing one, you should not let the HTML generating features make the choice for you. In the current freelance market, you will probably do much more business in book indexing.

FURTHER READING

Browne, Glenda. "HTML/Prep: Transforming Indexes for the Web." *Online Currents*, Vol.17 Issue 7, September 2002. www.webindexing.biz/articles/HTMLPrep.htm

Lamb, James A. Converting Indexes from Other Software. In *Website Indexes: Visitors to Content in Two Clicks*. Ardleigh, England: Jalamb.com Ltd., 2006.

Ream, David K. "Web Index Preparation with HTML/Prep." Leverage Technologies Inc., 2001. www.levtechinc.com/Resources/DKRArts/Art_wi.htm

SOFTWARE RESOURCES

CINDEX from Indexing Research, www.indexres.com

SKY Index Professional from SKY Software, www.sky-software.com

Macrex from Macrex Indexing Services, www.macrex.com

wINDEX from Susan Holbert Indexing Services, www.abbington.com/holbert/ windex.html

Mapper utility from Leverage Technologies, Inc., www.levtechinc.com/ProdServ/ LTUtils/Mapper.htm

HTML/Prep from Leverage Technologies, Inc., www.levtechinc.com/ProdScrv/ LTUtils/HTMLPrep.htm

XRefHT from Tim Craven, Freeware, publish.uwo.ca/%7Ecraven/freeware.htm

ADDITIONAL REFERENCES

Because there is little published literature on how to create HTML indexes in dedicated book indexing software, some of the information for this chapter comes from direct e-mail correspondence received in November 2006 from each of the following software vendors or representatives: Gale Rhoades regarding Macrex, Kamm Schreiner regarding SKY Index, and David Ream regarding HTML/Prep in general and its use with CINDEX in particular.

Chapter 5

XRefHT for Creating Web Indexes

As we have seen in the last chapter, converting an index created in dedicated book indexing software into HTML has the drawbacks of involving multiple steps, multiple software, and additional skills in using HTML editing software. Using standalone Web indexing software, such as XRefHT or HTML Indexer, allows you to use just a single software program for the entire process and requires almost no post-editing of the HTML index. The disadvantages are that the indexing capabilities are not as strong, and you cannot simultaneously create the same index for print. Standalone Web indexing software is designed for indexing existing Web sites, intranets, or portions of sites. This chapter will cover XRefHT, and Chapter 6 will take up the software HTML Indexer.

BACKGROUND

XRefHT, commonly pronounced "shreft," is a little-known but quite effective freeware indexing tool developed in 1998. Its name represents the two elements of "cross-references" and "hypertext." It was developed by and continues to be maintained by Timothy Craven, a professor of information science at the University of Western Ontario. His research specialties are computer-assisted abstracting, indexing, and thesaurus construction, so XRefHT and a related thesaurus construction software program were university-funded academic projects of his. Using XRefHT, in conjunction with the thesaurus tool, continues to be an assignment in the graduate level courses he teaches. An example of a Web site index created with this program appears online for the Birkbeck College of the University of London at www.bbk.ac.uk/help/index.

The software can be downloaded from publish.uwo.ca/%7Ecraven/freeware.htm for free, where the 32-bit Windows zipped program, XRefHT32, is listed as xrefht33.exe, and the Java 2 Platform Standard Edition (J2SE) program is listed as xrefthj.jar. The XRefHT Java version can run on any platform, including Macintosh and Linux, as long as you also have the Java Runtime Environment (freely downloadable). A documentation file comes with either version of the XRefHT download, which briefly explains the individual menu functions but unfortunately does not describe the procedure for creating an index. It is that process which this chapter explains. Although the screenshot examples in this chapter come from XRefH32 for Windows, XRefHT for Java functions just the same.

EXTRACTING WEB PAGE DATA

When you launch the program, the interface you will see is shown in Figure 5.1.

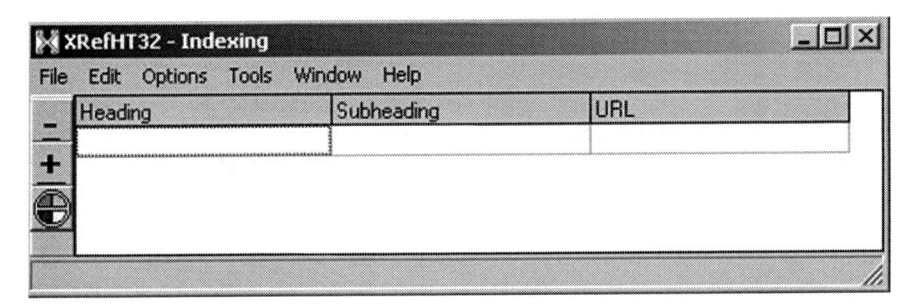

Figure 5.1

"Heading" designates the main entry, "Subheading" is used for the subentry, and "URL" is used for the locator. (Sub-subentries are not supported.) The spreadsheet nature of the interface thus bears a slight resemblance to that of SKY Index. Usually the URL is simply the Web page file name, such as "contact.htm," but it can additionally include the folder name, if the site has subfolders, and it can also include anchor names within pages. A complete URL for an external Web site link can also be entered in this field. All columns can be resized, and the entire window can be resized to the maximum size of your monitor display.

Extracting Page Titles with URLs

Although you can manually type in the index entries and the corresponding URLs, it is not necessary to do so since you are working from pages already in electronic form. You can load, or "extract," the pertinent information from the Web pages into the program. The URLs are for individual pages in the Web site, and each Web page typically has a title. When you extract URLs for Web pages, the associated page title, if any, is extracted along with the URL. The following steps assume that the Web site files are on your computer, not on a remote server out on the Internet. While it is possible to index pages on the Internet, their page titles and anchors must be extracted for each page one at a time, so it is not very practical to do so.

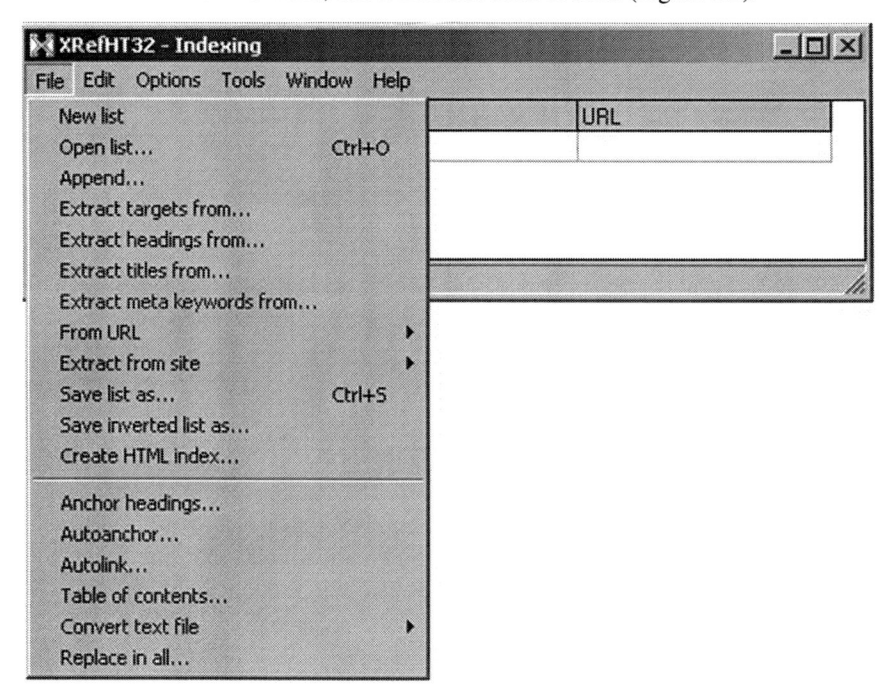

1. From the **File** menu, select **Extract titles from...** (Figure 5.2).

Figure 5.2

2. Browse your computer for the folder containing the files of the Web site to be indexed. Select all the files to be considered for indexing (excluding the images, for example). If your site has multiple subfolders, you need to select each subfolder individually and then select the files within the subfolder. Remember, by clicking in the window and then typing **CTRL+A** you can select all of the files at once.

   You have the option of limiting your selection by **Files of Type**, and you could choose just HTML files, rather than All files. This would exclude the image files. However, in some Web sites, Web pages are created with technology other than simple HTML and have file extensions such as .php, .jsp, or .asp. If you choose just HTML files, you will exclude these other files. However, you will definitely want these pages to index, if they are part of the site. While some of these files may turn out to be inappropriate (such as a login confirmation page), others may be suitable for indexing (such as a login page itself).

3. After selecting the files, click on **Open**.
4. The **URL Prefix** window pops up. You need to enter a folder name here only if your Web site has subfolders and you have selected files within a

subfolder. If this is the case, type in the subfolder name followed by a forward slash, for example, **articles/**. Click on **OK**. The process of selecting files has to be repeated for each subfolder. If your site has no subfolders (except perhaps for images, which you will not index anyway), then you may leave the URL Prefix field blank and click **Cancel**.

You should then see all of the selected files added to your XRefHT program window list. File names are added to the URL field. Page titles, where they exist, are automatically added to the Heading field. You then replace the page titles with the main entries in your index. These page titles should be considered as the means to identify the Web pages only, rather than as suggested index entries. For example, page titles may start with the name of the organization, which would not be helpful in an index.

Extracting Web Page Named Anchors

When indexing a Web site, you are not limited to creating locators for the pages, but you may also drill down to the level of sections within a page. Thus your indexing can be more specific, and the hyperlinked entries will jump directly to the appropriate section within the page and not merely to the top of the page. These lower level sections may have a named anchor preceding the section heading. Therefore, as a second step, named anchors, also called "Targets," should be extracted where they exist.

1. From the **File** menu, select **Extract targets from...** (also Figure 5.2).
2. Go to the same folder containing all the files of the Web site to be indexed. Select all the files to be considered for indexing. You probably won't know which files contain named anchors, though, so select them all after clicking in the window pane (**CTRL+A**).
3. Click on **Open**.
5. When the **URL Prefix** window pops up, enter the appropriate subfolder name, if any, and click on **OK**. If the Web site has no subfolders, then leave this field blank and click on either **OK** or **Cancel**.

The URLs for any anchors will now automatically be appended to your existing list of Headings and URLs. You can recognize the URLs with anchors, as they have a crosshatch symbol, #, between the page name and the anchor name.

If there is any text between the named anchor target and the closing </a> link tag, such as `<a name="books">Books</a>`, the text, in this case "books," is automatically entered into the Heading field.

Since it is not necessary to enclose text for an anchor to be functional, it may appear as follows:

```
<a name="books"></a>Books
```

In this case, no text will automatically be entered into the Heading field. More often than not, anchor tags do not surround any text. Sometimes only the first word of a heading somehow gets included before the closing </a> link tag, so the automatically generated text may include only part of the heading.

When there are named anchors, the title of the page is automatically entered into the Subheading field. This default insertion of titles as Subheadings can be turned off by unchecking "Title a subhead" in the Options menu (**Options > List insertion > Title as subhead**). The page title is really no more suitable as a subentry than it is as a main entry, and its usefulness in the extraction is mainly for identifying the page.

In the screenshot shown in Figure 5.3, page titles have been extracted as Headings, and then the targets (named anchors) have been extracted and appended to the list (only partially displaying). The page titles were automatically entered as the Subheadings. Because no text was within the anchor tags, the Heading field for these URLs was left blank.

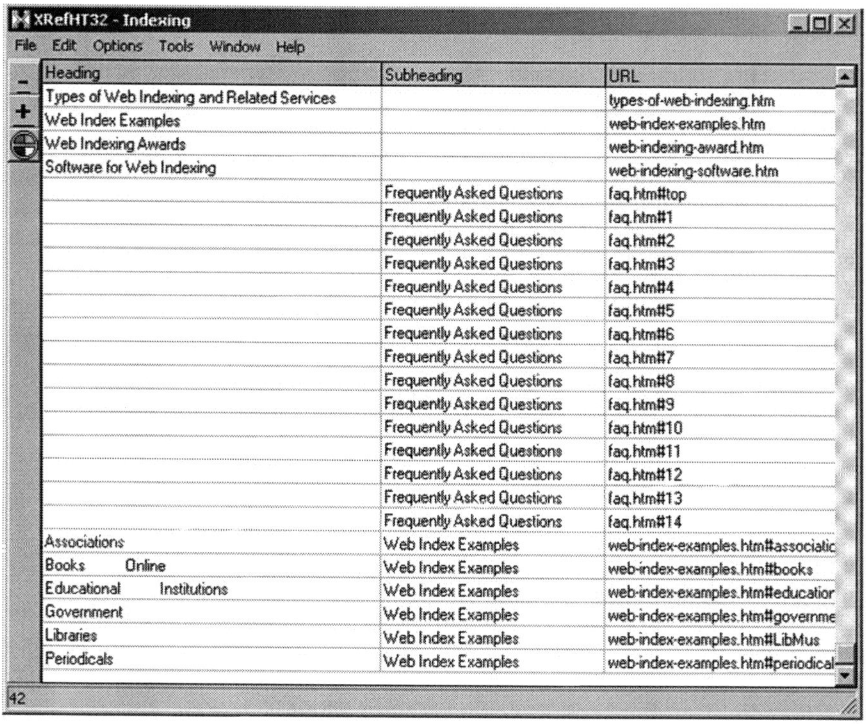

Figure 5.3

Often there will be extracted targets that are not useful for indexing, such as internal back-to-the-top-of-the-page links, which might look like this: events.htm#top. You can simply delete these rows from your list.

Extracting Headings Lacking Anchors

Web sites do not consistently use anchors. Sometimes the anchors are insufficient or totally omitted. Therefore, as an indexer, you will inevitably find sections of a Web page under headings with specific indexable content, but without an anchor. XRefHT takes this into account and provides a feature for adding all Web page headings to the list of Headings for indexing. XRefHT takes advantage of the HTML heading tag codes of H1, H2, H3, ..., which are used as follows: <h2>Main Topic</h2>.

These HTML headings can automatically be added to the list of Headings. (Again, the page titles will automatically be entered as the Subheadings, if you leave the default option "Titles as subheads" selected under **Options > List insertion**.) The URL, however, is left incomplete. What XRefHT does is add the page URL with the # sign but without a named anchor following it. You will still have to create the named anchor at each heading you choose to index.

The procedure for extracting headings follows the same steps as for extracting target anchors:

1. From the **File** menu, select **Extract headings from...**

2. Go to the same folder containing all the files of the Web site to be indexed. Again, select all the files to be considered for indexing. You probably won't know which files contain headings, so select them all (**CTRL+A**).

3. Click on **Open**. A small box appears allowing you to refine your selection of heading levels. The default is to accept all heading levels, and I recommend that you accept all heading levels. Heading levels may have been applied in an inconsistent manner, and it is better to have too many and remove some from the indexing than to miss some that should have been included. (It is the same principle as in book indexing, that it is always easier to trim an index down at the end as opposed to beefing it up.)

4. When the **URL Prefix** window pops up, enter the appropriate subfolder name, if any, and click on **OK**. If the Web site has no subfolders, then leave this field blank and click on either **OK** or **Cancel**.

The partial URLs for any headings (excluding the future unnamed anchor) will now automatically be appended to your existing list of Headings and URLs. You may now create index terms in association with any of these additional headings and the page subsections that they denote. For the index entries to link to these additional headings, though, you still need to create the anchor in the Web page file and fill in the anchor name next to the # in the URL field of XRefHT. If the number of anchors to add is not too great, you can create them by editing the Web pages in your HTML editing software. If it turns out that there are many headings to which you want to add anchors, or if you are unable to or unskilled at creating the anchors yourself, then you may prefer to use XRefHT's Anchor feature explained in the next section.

ADDING ANCHORS

One of the unique features of XRefHT is that it will automatically insert named anchors at headings in Web pages that lack anchors. You specify the file(s) and the software goes in and adds anchors with the names derived from the text of the heading. The entire text between the pair of heading codes repeats itself in the name of the anchor, with the addition of underscores in blank spaces, such as:

    <h3>Drawbacks of fulltext search</h3>

changes to:

    <h3><A NAME="Drawbacks_of_fulltext_search">Drawbacks of
    fulltext search</a></h3>

After you have extracted the headings, you should decide which Web pages have headings that seem to be good candidates for indexing locators but lack anchors, because adding anchors is done one page at a time. Here are the steps for this process:

1. From File menu select **File > Anchor headings**. In the directory of files that appear, select the file for the desired Web page. "Select all" will not work for this feature. If multiple files need anchors added, then you will need to repeat the steps that follow.

2. Click on **Open**. You will have the option of saving the file with the same name or with a new name. In general, it's not a practical idea to rename the files of your Web site, so I would recommend saving it as is, without a new name. Simply double-click on the same file again, and it will automatically be placed into the File Name field, and then it replaces the existing file of the same name. You might choose, however, to save a file with a different name, if you are just testing the feature of adding anchors.

3. Click on **Save**.

4. Click on **OK** when the Autoanchor **Text for Links** box pops up, even if you leave the box blank. (Clicking Cancel cancels the entire operation.) Entering something here is an option in cases where there are more than one occurrence of a given heading or term in the source file. This is not necessary for indexing, but could be an aid to navigation within a page. It

is rare, though, that you would have more than one identical heading on the same page. For the most part, you can ignore this feature.

5. Select **Extract targets from...** and choose the file for which you just automatically added anchors to the headings.

6. Assuming you had previously extracted these same headings before they had anchors added to them, you may now delete those entries that lack the anchors since they are simply duplicates. (How to delete is explained in the next section, Editing the Index.)

It may appear that some strange anchor names get automatically inserted. Since the anchor name is derived from everything between the pair of heading tags, it might include other tags, such as those for font, and have extra blank spaces displaying with an underscore, as in the following actual example:

```
<A NAME="_font_face=_Georgia,_Times_New_Roman,_Times,_
serif___ br____ Web_Site_Database_Administrator_/font_">
```

If the site designer had used a style sheet, then the specifications for font would not need to be indicated in the body of the page within heading codes. If you see these types of anchor names generated, you either have to accept them as they appear, or edit them to make them identical in both places: in the source Web page file and in the index URL you are working on in the XRefHT program. Yet, even with these long, strange names, the anchors will still work. It is advisable to proceed with indexing before you edit any anchors, because it may turn out that you don't want to index to the odd-named anchor in the first place. If you end up deleting an index entry with one of these new anchors, you don't have to delete the anchor in the text, but you might choose to, if it is extremely long, simply for a cleaner coding.

You need to consider carefully what to index and what not to index. If you were adding anchors by hand, you would not create so many. Not every heading should have an anchor. The topic of deciding what to include in the index is covered in Chapter 7.

Autoanchor

Autoanchor is another option in the File menu. It also automatically adds anchors to a selected Web page file. Instead of adding anchors at headings, Autoanchor will add anchors at any instance of certain words within the text. These words are derived from the existing index headings (main entries) and then matched to words in the text. Although this is an interesting feature, I do not recommend using it when indexing Web pages. It tends to insert far more anchors than needed for useful indexing. Users of Web indexes expect to be taken to the top of a page or partway down a page to a heading, but not to the middle of text with no heading viewable in the screen display.

EDITING THE INDEX

When editing your list of index entries with URLs, it's a good idea to periodically save it by selecting from the menu **File > Save list as** (**CTRL+S**). The saved XRefHT file, which is not yet a generated HTML index, will have the extension **.anc,** which stands for an Anchor file, and is referred to in the XRefHT menus as a "list." You may reopen such a list file in XRefHT in a later work session. XRefHT cannot keep multiple documents open, however, so if you open a new list while working on another one, XRefHT will prompt you to save changes to your currently open list.

To edit the contents of a cell in the grid, select it by either double-clicking on it or using the arrow keys or the mouse (single click) to select a cell and then press Enter.

To delete an index entry line, after inserting your cursor in the line, you can choose from three methods:

1. Select **Edit > Delete item** from the menu.
2. Type **CTRL+backspace**.
3. Click on the minus sign (-) that is in the upper left-hand corner of the window, as shown in the screenshot in Figure 5.4.

To add a new blank line in order to add an entry, place your cursor in the line below where the new line is to be added. You can then choose from three methods:

1. Select **Edit > Insert** item from the menu.
2. Type **CTRL+space**.
3. Click on the plus sign (+) that is in the upper left-hand corner of the window, as shown in the screenshot in Figure 5.4 (minus sign for deleting; plus sign for adding).

If you have automatically added all target anchors in all headings, you will obviously want to delete a number of these entry lines as inappropriate. Meanwhile, you

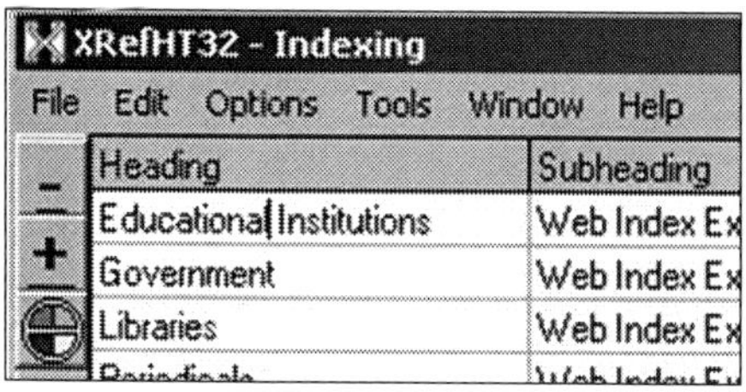

Figure 5.4

will also want to add index entry lines in order to add variant terms (double posting) that point to the same URL. It really does not matter where you enter the new entries in the index, for the index will be automatically sorted alphabetically afterward. Unlike dedicated indexing software, you are not working in a sorted order. Sorting is a separate step here.

Indexing Process

Typically, indexers create an index from scratch rather than editing one that is automatically generated. It requires a slightly different perspective on the project to edit an automatically generated index.

The basic approach, in any case, is to have both your Web browser open, with the Web page to view, and XRefHT open to edit the index. In your Web browser, browse to view the home page of the Web site on your computer, through **File > Open File**. Then select the URL from the XRefHT list (starting with the first and working your way down), and then copy and paste it into the latter part of the URL in your browser (retaining the preceding file path). View the page (or page section, if using an anchor) and decide how it should best be indexed. Then, back in XRefHT, replace/edit the automatically generated Heading (main entry) and Subheading (subentry) fields for that URL. Create additional index entries for the same URL as desired. Then move on to the next URL in the list.

You may notice that XRefHT has a simple Web browser of its own built in (selected from **Window > Web browser**), but its effectiveness is limited. You can use it to add the URLs to the index list of individual Web pages as they are visited. This may be practical only for indexing external Web site URLs, rather than the pages within a site. Extracting titles, anchors, and headings is a much more practical method of indexing a Web site.

Editing Tips

If you want to use any automatically generated index entry, remember that you may need to replace all default title capitalization of terms that are not proper nouns in the entries with lowercase, depending on the style of you index. Chances are, though, that you will end up completely retyping any automatically generated index entries.

Not every URL will automatically generate a Heading (main entry), such as when the site designer forgot to create a page title, but every line must have a Heading. So, make sure that you either add Headings (main entries) to URLs that lack them or delete the entire row.

Many URLs should have a second or third index entry to serve the user as an additional entry point (also called double posting). Unlike commercial book indexing software, XRefHT does not offer an efficient way to do this. You cannot duplicate index entries for editing, nor can you automatically invert (or "flip") headings (main entries) and subentries. This is the main weakness of XRefHT. Instead, you

XRefHT for Creating Web Indexes   71

Heading	Subheading	URL
product safety testing		prod-test-essai/index_e.html
product safety testing	testing methods	prod-test-essai/method/index_
product safety testing	testing methods: chemistry	prod-test-essai/method/chem-(
product safety testing	testing methods: flammability	prod-test-essai/method/inflamn
product safety testing	testing methods: mechanical engineering	prod-test-essai/method/engin-i
product safety testing	testing programs	prod-test-essai/program.html
product safety testing	testing services	prod-test-essai/services.html

Figure 5.5

must insert a line, select the text to be duplicated from another index line, copy and paste it into the new index entry line, and then edit it as needed. For the high-speed user of dedicated book indexing software, this can seem rather time-consuming.

Sub-Subentries

Since XRefHT does not support more than two levels of index entries, to designate sub-subentries you must resort writing the sub-subentries on the same line followed by a character such as a colon or a dash. An example using colons appears in the screenshot shown in Figure 5.5.

This will result in index entries displaying as follows:

product safety testing
- testing methods
- testing methods: chemistry
- testing methods: flammability
- testing methods: mechanical engineering
- testing services

You can also edit the index using your HTML editor to create indented sub-subentries.

Creating Cross-References

For cross-references, you have two possible approaches: references that link directly to the Web page with the content (the preferred option if there are no subentries) and references that jump to another term within the index (the preferred option when there are subentries).

A drawback is that XRefHT will only create one hyperlinked entry per line, and the entire line will be hypertext. Thus, for a *See* reference you cannot create a nonlinked entry with a hypertext-linked cross-reference following it on the same line, and for a *See also* reference you cannot create a hyperlinked term to one destination followed by another hyperlinked term to a different destination. The following examples, where the underlined text is hypertext, *cannot* be generated by XRefHT:

    cars. *See* <u>automobiles</u>　　　　<u>cars</u>. *See also* <u>transportation</u>

Instead, either the entire line will be hypertext to the same destination (which is acceptable for *See* references but not for *See also* references) or the cross-reference has to be put on another line, below and indented, like a subentry.

When creating a *See* reference that links directly to the Web page with the content, you utilize the automatically entered URL and type the cross-reference in either the Heading or the Subheading field. If you type the entire cross-reference line in the Heading field, the cross-reference in the generated index will stay on the same line with the entire line hypertext, as in the following example, where the underlined text is hypertext:

    <u>cars. See automobiles</u>

If you type the first term of the cross-reference in the Heading field and the cross-reference in the Subheading field, the cross-reference in the generated index will appear on a separate, indented line, as in the following example, where the underlined text is hypertext:

    cars
        <u>See automobiles</u>

If it is important for your index style to have the entry appear as **cars.** *See* **automobiles**, then you should create the cross-reference on a second line and then edit the generated HTML index afterward in your HTML editing program to combine the two lines into one.

When creating a *See also* reference that links directly to the Web page with the content, first create a duplicate entry for the first term of the reference. This way, the Heading remains hypertext to its destination, and the *See also* reference is hypertext to a different destination. One line will link to the original URL, and the second line will be the cross-reference. For the cross-reference line, type the reference in the Subheading field and type the new URL for the referenced term's page in the URL field, as in the screenshot in Figure 5.6.

This index output will look like this:

    <u>Cars</u>
        <u>See also transportation</u>

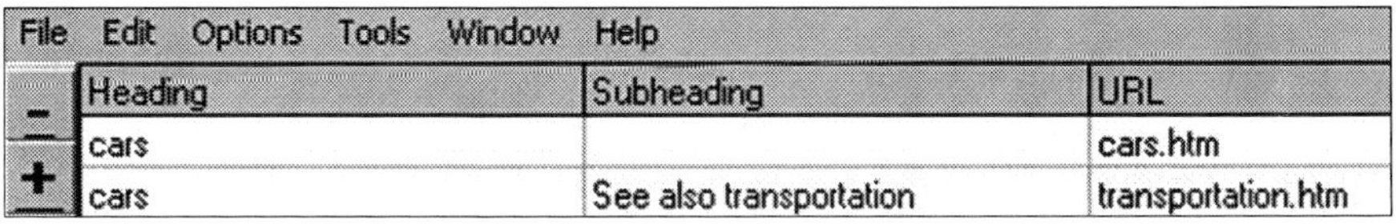

	Heading	Subheading	URL
−	cars		cars.htm
+	cars	See also transportation	transportation.htm

Figure 5.6

As with the *See* reference, if you desire the cross-reference to appear all on a single line, you will have to edit the HTML page in your HTML editor afterward.

When creating a *See* or *See also* reference that jumps to the referenced term within the index (preferred when the referenced term has subentries), the URL must be an anchor within the index page, rather than a destination page URL. Fortunately, XRefHT automatically creates anchors at every main entry within the index, just in case you plan to make an entry the destination of a cross-reference. You merely have to type the anchor name in the URL field. The anchor name that XRefHT automatically creates is the name of the entry in all caps and with underscores instead of spaces. Therefore, if you created a main entry of **accreditation training**, its anchor will be #ACCREDITATION_TRAINING.

The screenshot in Figure 5.7 illustrates how to create different kinds of cross-references in XRefHT.

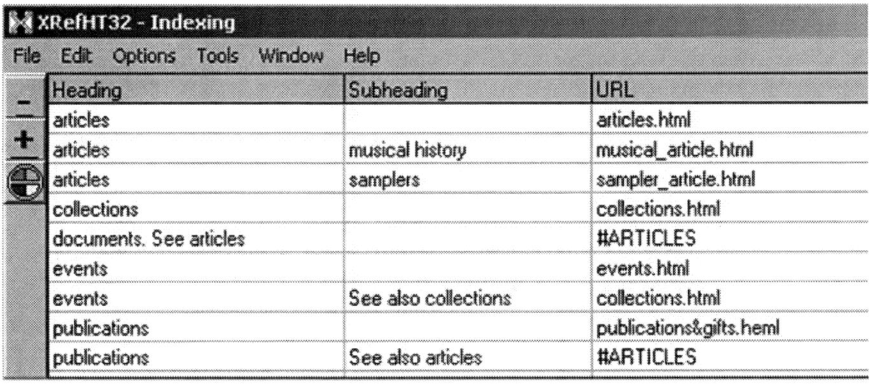

XRefHT32 - Indexing

	Heading	Subheading	URL
−	articles		articles.html
+	articles	musical history	musical_article.html
⊕	articles	samplers	sampler_article.html
	collections		collections.html
	documents. See articles		#ARTICLES
	events		events.html
	events	See also collections	collections.html
	publications		publications&gifts.heml
	publications	See also articles	#ARTICLES

Figure 5.7

Since the main entry **articles** has subentries under it, the cross-references pointing to it link to the term within the index rather than to the indexed page.

Sorting the Index

After completing the indexing, sort the index entries alphabetically by Heading to check them over for any duplicate or near duplicate main entries. (The sorting is word-by-word, and there is no option to sort letter-by-letter.) Since XRefHT lacks the typing memory found in commercial dedicated indexing software, you can easily write inconsistent entries, such as typing a term in the singular once and in the plural a second time. By alphabetically sorting the list of entries, you will be able to catch these errors. In the **Edit** menu, select **Sort**. This will sort the list alphabetically by Heading. If you subsequently edit or add Headings, you can select **Sort** again in order to sort the list again. Once you have sorted the list by Heading, you may also resort by URL again.

There is no way to make XRefHT generically ignore characters in the sort (such as articles at the start of titles of works), although there are ways of overriding the sort for specific entries. In the specific case of quotation marks in an entry, such as for the title of an article, you can make XRefHT ignore quotation marks in the sort, yet display them in the index entry, if you type in the HTML code for quotation marks, which is “ for an opening quote and ” for the closing quote.

For example, rather than typing the following into the Heading field:

"Organizing Your Site from A–Z"

you should type the following:

“Organizing Your Site from A–Z”

If you wish to override the default alphabetical sorting, such as to sort by dates in some instances, you can specify prefixes and definitions for how XRefHT should sort them and save these in a text file. Then, call up this file for sort key lookup under **Options > Sort keys…**

Find/Replace

In the **Edit** menu, there is a basic **Find/Replace** feature (**CTRL+F**). It works on all three fields: Heading, Subheading, and URL. Since the URLs have no spaces and often lack capitalization in them, you can phrase a Find/Replace with spaced and capital letters so that it will find and replace text only in the Heading and Subheading fields.

Spell Check

XRefHT even has a spell-check feature, which is found under the **Tools** menu. You spell check as a step at the end, rather than having interactive spell checking as you type. The dictionary is American English, and the current version of the spell checker, VisualSpeller, does not support custom dictionaries, so you cannot add words. It is possible, though, to install and use additional dictionaries as .vtd files for British English and other European languages. What is nice about the spell checker, though, is that it operates only on the Heading and Subheading field, not the URL field, which inevitably contains unconventional spelling.

GENERATING THE WEB INDEX

Before generating the index, it is a good idea to save the list one more time. You may need to reopen the ungenerated index .anc file to add indexing entries to your index for a new or revised Web page for future updates.

Index Options

Prior to generating the index, you might also want to check and modify any of the index options. From the **Options** menu, select **HTML index creation** where the following options are available:

- **Include cross-references** – This will implement cross-references based on a thesaurus created in a currently running copy of TheW32, another freeware program by Tim Craven. If you are not using the thesaurus tool TheW32, leave this option unselected. Instead, create cross-references by the method explained earlier.
- **Split by initials** – If selected, XRefHT will automatically create a separate Web page for each letter section of the alphabet, in addition to the general index page. Use this option if the index turns out to be very long.
- **Allow headings as links** – Usually this should be checked. If not, only subentries, and not main entries, will be linked.
- **Run in subheadings** – This index style, frequently found in the indexes of scholarly books, is generally employed to save space. Since space is not an issue on Web pages, avoid this option. However, it might be a practical choice for Web-based periodical indexes containing multiple short "subheadings" consisting only of issue dates.

Generating the Index

To create the index, select from the **File** menu, **Create HTML index...** .

Give the index file a name (not index.htm or index.html, of course, which are reserved for the home page) and save it in the same folder as the home page of your Web site. In the current version of XRefHT (1.1, Release 6, Build 4, December 5, 2006), you have to type in the file extension of .htm or .html, because picking the file extension from the **Save as type** list does not have an effect.

If you have selected the option of splitting the index into separate letter files, you do not have to worry about naming each file; names with the letters will be automatically generated.

Figure 5.8 shows an excerpt of a short index generated by XRefHT illustrating the default style.

As you can see in the figure, the formatting uses unordered lists. For a discussion of ordered vs. unordered lists, see the sections on lists in Chapters 2 and 3.

You cannot set any preferences in the index style or format, but you can change it by hand in your HTML editing software afterward. For example, you may want

Index

A B C D E F G H I J K L M N O P Q R S T U V W X Y Z

A

- about web indexing
- application form for members
- article on web indexing

C

- contact information
- contract indexer database
  - login page

D

- database of contract indexers

Figure 5.8

to change the font style or color, change the wording and appearance of the page heading **Index**, or remove the bullets with a style sheet instruction.

Generating a Keyword Index

There is an additional option under the **File** menu of **Extract meta keywords from...** . Meta keywords are what a Web site creator assigns (with the meta keyword tag) to the non-displayable head section of each Web page so that the page will be retrieved by search engines when people search on these keywords. XRefHT also provides the option to generate an index based on these keywords, instead of creating terms for each page and named anchor as explained in the preceding sections. This is a different approach to Web site indexing and it is more akin to periodical database indexing than back-of-the-book indexing. Prior to creating the index, you need to add meta keywords to the head section of each Web page in a consistent manner, perhaps by using a controlled vocabulary.

CONCLUSION

XRefHT's ability to extract headings and automatically add anchors is a powerful and unique feature in Web site indexing tools, but it should not be misused. It is a good idea to extract the headings to see what they are, but it might not always be a good idea to add anchors to all of them. If only a few headings should have anchors added, it might be more practical to add them manually to avoid adding numerous, strange, lengthy anchor names to the file. For one who has no skills in creating anchors, though, this automated feature could prove quite helpful.

As an indexing tool, however, XRefHT lacks some of the term editing features of the commercial indexing tools of CINDEX, Macrex, or SKY Index (whose indexes can be converted to HTML) and of the Web indexing tool HTML Indexer, which will be described in Chapter 6. Also, the process of creating cross-references is not fully automated. There is also the drawback that subfolders of files to be indexed have to be added individually for extracting. As such, XRefHT may be more practical with smaller rather than with larger sites.

FURTHER READING

Hedden, Heather. "HTML Indexing Freeware: XRefHT32." *Key Words*, Vol. 13, No. 4, October–December, 2005, pp. 141–142.

Lamb, James. *Website Indexes: Visitors to Content in Two Clicks*. Ardleigh, Essex, England: Jalamb.com Ltd., 2006. Available at www.lulu.com/content/300848

SOFTWARE RESOURCES

XRefHT from Tim Craven Freeware, publish.uwo.ca/%7Ecraven/freeware.htm
VisualSpeller Standard British, Czech, Dutch, French, German and Italian Dictionaries, www.ouisoft.com/calypsospell.htm

Chapter 6

HTML Indexer for Creating Web Indexes

HTML Indexer is the only commercially marketed, stand-alone, dedicated Web site indexing tool available at the time of this writing. How it works and what it can do is somewhat similar to XRefHT. It extracts Web page file names and also anchors within pages and their URLs. It does not extract headings, though, nor does it automatically add anchors to headings. This may or may not be important for your projects. Creating additional index entries is easier and more sophisticated than in XRefHT. HTML Indexer does not require a separate thesaurus tool to automatically create cross-references. Finally, you have many more options in HTML Indexer to control the formatting and output of the index, without having to manually change the code. With HTML Indexer, a commercial product, unlike XRefHT, you can also count on getting technical support to answer any question. In addition to standard online help documentation, HTML Indexer also comes with a Tutorial that even includes sample files. For examples of indexes created with the program, you can go to the Customer Examples page of the HTML Indexer site, finitesite.com/info/Examples.htm.

HTML Indexer was developed and is marketed by David M. Brown, a technical writer and former documentation manager, through his own consultancy, Brown Inc., in Portland, Oregon. Since his specialty is writing online help, he was interested in creating a better tool for writing online help indexes. As such, HTML Indexer is a tool not only for creating Web site indexes but also for creating indexes for HTML Help, JavaHelp, and other HTML documents. In addition to supporting HTML Indexer, Brown also continues to write online documentation and provides training in this area. HTML Indexer's first public release was in 1998, and the latest major version, 4.0, appeared in 2002. Brown continues to release minor updates to the program.

HTML Indexer costs $239.95 as of early 2007. You may download a free demo of HTML Indexer from its Web site, www.html-indexer.com. The demonstration version fortunately has no time limit. Its only limitation is that you cannot save the index entries or project settings between sessions. You can still generate an index file, as long as you create it in one session, keeping the program running and computer turned on.

ADDING FILES TO A PROJECT

When you launch the program, you get a blank gray window with a menu at the top:

1. Select from the menu **File > New (CTRL+N)** or use the **New** icon/button from the button bar. A window, **Browse for Folder, Select Project Directory,** will appear.
2. Browse to select the folder in which your Web site files are saved and click on **Open**.

You will see the following features in Figure 6.1:

- An index project receives the default name of Indexer.ipj (changing the default name is explained later under "Saving").
- The blank gray window becomes white and is tiled into two panes.
- The left-hand pane has a directory of folders. It starts with a folder called HTML Indexer project. Within it are three subfolders: one for your Web site pages, one for External URLs, and one for X-ref (cross-reference) Locators.
- The right pane has columns for Index Entry and Target URL.
- Additionally a window has popped up for "Add Files to Project."

Adding Pages, Anchors, and URLs

Unlike XRefHT, URLs of both Web page file names and anchor targets are extracted into the indexing program in a single step. Subfolders are also extracted, so the entire site can be extracted at once. Additional unanchored headings, however, cannot be extracted. In the **Add Files to Project** window, select the folder on your computer in which the Web site pages are located and click on **Add**. After you have added the files, you may close this window.

You do not have any choice here as to what kinds of files to add, though. HTML Indexer assumes any file with the extension .htm, .html, or .asp is an HTML source file. You can expand this list to include other extensions, such as .php or .shtml, as well, but it requires editing the INI file associated with the HTML Indexer program. The instructions for doing this are on the HTML Indexer site, "Tips and Techniques: Include HTML Files with Other Extensions" (www.finitesite.com/info/Tips.htm# types). Whatever the file extension, the files still must be in HTML format, beginning with an <HTML> tag and ending with an </HTML> tag.

HTML Indexer for Creating Web Indexes 81

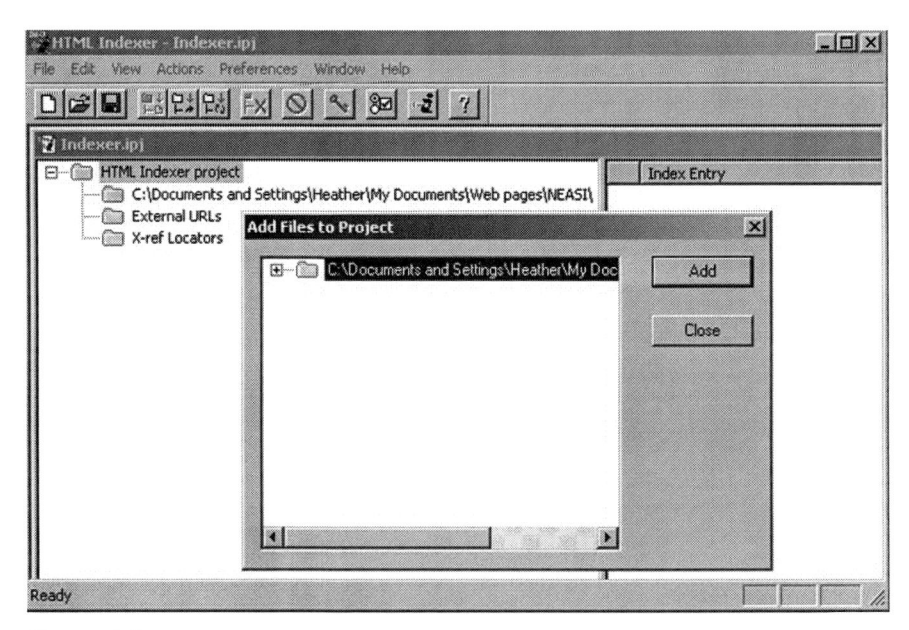

Figure 6.1

Indexing Non-HTML Files

You might also wish to index files that are not at all in HTML format, such as PDFs (portable document format files), PowerPoint presentations, graphics, or video files. You may add such files to your index project through a different method, the **Add External URLs** function, which is under the **Actions** menu. The Actions menu will only appear after you have added HTML files to a project. Assuming all files from the Web site reside on your computer in your file management system, such as Windows Explorer, open the list of all the Web site files and sort by file type to identify the PDFs or other files to be included. If you notice any appropriate PDFs or other files, type each file name (or copy and paste) into the field of the **Add External URLs to Project** box and add them one by one. If the file names have spaces in them, rename the files first. These are the steps to follow for adding the URLs:

1. In HTML Indexer, from the menu select **Actions > Add External URLs...** or select the **Add External URLs** icon/button from the button menu.
2. In the **Add External URLs to Project** box that pops up, type or copy and paste the copied file name.
3. Click on the **Add** button or hit **<Enter>** to add the URL.
4. Repeat for each file.

It is not necessary to open the files that you are adding to the index project. Type only the file name, not a complete URL as would be required for true external links. Don't let the designation "external URLs" confuse you. What is important to note is that the URLs for these non-HTML pages will be kept separately in the project folder labeled **External URLs** and not in the folder for the Web site, which the next section describes. They can be indexed just the same, though.

Project Tree Pane

Following the extraction of Web page URLs, you will notice in the main window a plus sign added to the folder for your Web site (the top of the three subfolders in the left pane). If you click once on the plus sign, the folder will expand to show in the left pane, called the Project Tree pane (Figure 6.2), all the subfolders (if any) and all the HTML files in the folder. The subfolders and the files are arranged in alphabetical order by title.

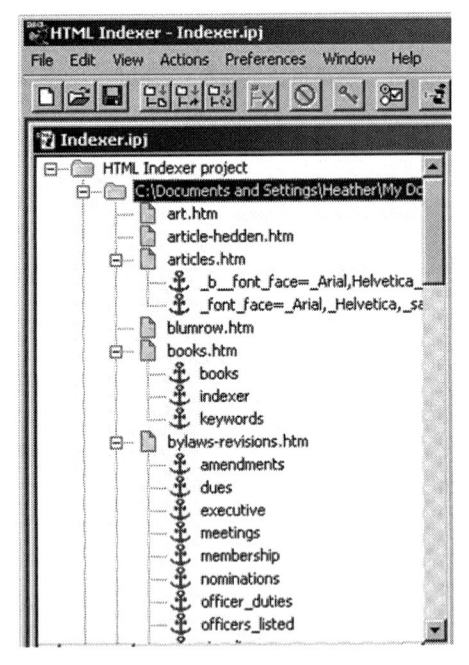

Figure 6.2

If there are subfolders, they will have plus signs next to them, which you may click once in order to expand the contents of the subfolder and see the list of files within it.

Some of these files, in turn, have plus signs next to them. This is to indicate that the file has internal anchors. If you click once on the plus sign, the file expands to display the named anchors within the file. Each is preceded by a small icon of a ship's anchor.

Any item selected in the left pane by clicking once on its icon, rather than on the plus/minus sign, calls up a list of URLs in the right pane. It is in this left Project Tree pane that you will select the files and anchors for indexing. You may also pick them from here to view in your browser when deciding how to index.

Index Entry Pane

In the right pane (see Figure 6.3), three columns appear. In the first column the icons indicate the source of the URL, which can be a Web page or an anchor. The small notation <**H1**, next to the page icon, indicates text extracted from a heading. The notation <**Ti** indicates text extracted from the title, and the notation <**A** indicates text extracted from between anchor tags (which often does not even occur, as anchor tags need not surround any text).

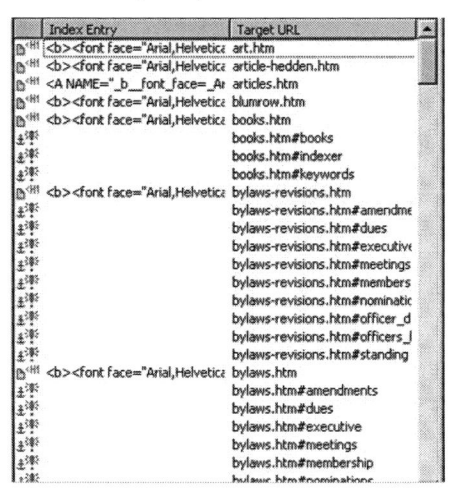

Figure 6.3

The second column contains the Index Entry, which may have text that you will want to replace. If there is no automatically generated text for the Index Entry, as usually happens with anchors, then a fat, red exclamation mark appears.

The third column is for the Target URL, which is the Web page name or the page name with an anchor. If there are subfolders, the folder paths will also be included in the URL.

You will notice the absence of a subentry column. Subentries are entered as part of the main entries and are set off by commas.

Unlike XRefHT, the default text automatically entered in the Index Entry field is not the Web page title, but rather the contents between the first pair of heading tags on the page. Only if there are no heading tags is the page title extracted here. As we discovered in Chapter 6, all kinds of formatting codes are likely to be found in the heading tags. Thus, the automatically generated index entries in HTML Indexer have less substance than those automatically generated in XRefHT. But since you will replace them during the indexing process, it does not matter that much. In fact, you don't even need to look at the Index Entry pane until after you have created some real index entries to replace the automatically generated ones.

You can resize the panes and windows. Watch out, though, as sometimes the scrollbar on the right pane can get cut off at the right, if the windows are not sized properly.

Saving

HTML Indexer has an unconventional way to save an index project with a new name. While you can select **Save** from the **File** menu (or use the **Save** icon/button from the button bar), it does not offer a "Save As" option. Instead, you must go to **Preferences > Set Filenames...** and replace the default Indexer.ipj name with a name of your choosing ending with the extension of .ipj. That extension stands for "index project." Since this name change is a preference setting, it will automatically be assigned to your next new index project until you change it the same way. Note that you cannot save your project file at all if you are using the free demo.

VIEWING PAGES AND INDEXING

One of the nice things about HTML Indexer, is that you can easily call up and view in your Web browser the pages you are indexing, without having to copy and paste the URLs. Similarly, you can call up Web pages to edit (namely add additional named anchors) in your chosen HTML editor.

First, under **Preferences > HTML Tools...** confirm the browser and HTML editor software you use (Figure 6.4). *Note*: This may not work with all browsers and editors, but it works fine with Internet Explorer as the browser.

When you start indexing, expand the file list in the left Project Tree pane:

1. Select the first file.
2. Select from the main menu **View > Selected Source File**, or right click and select **View Selected Source File**.
3. The Web page will then display in your browser program (in a new window) so that you can review the contents of the page before indexing it.
4. Close the browser window when done reading the page. Every time you select another page to view, another browser window opens, rather than

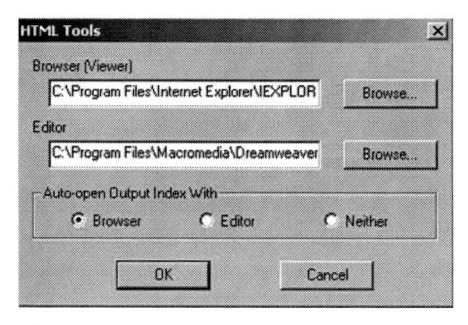

Figure 6.4

replacing the Web page last viewed. This means that soon you would have lots of browser windows open.

This ability to call up a URL from inside HTML Indexer to appear in your browser works for complete Web pages only, not for anchors within pages.

In the process of indexing, I suggest resizing the windows for each program of HTML Indexer and your browser to narrower widths and positioning them vertically next to each other in your monitor so you can see both programs at once. You will be selecting the pages and anchors from the left Project Tree pane, but you only need to view the start of the index entry in the right Index Entry pane, so both panes can be made quite narrow.

Adding Index Entries

After reviewing the page to be indexed in your browser, while it is still selected in the left Project Tree pane, you may add index entries.

If the file has anchors, you should first click on the plus sign to expand the file selection prior to assigning index terms. Otherwise, when you add an index entry, the indexing will automatically be added repeatedly to *all* the anchors within that page, something that you do not want. So, if there are anchors, after expanding them, first select the file icon for the entire web page to index (the page should be indexed as a whole, not just the anchors within it), then select each anchor individually to add individual index entries to each. In other words, index the anchors as if you were indexing separate pages. Keep in mind that the anchors are listed alphabetically by anchor name, not in the order in which they appear on the page. Here is the indexing procedure:

1. Select a file (after it is expanded) or an anchor in the left pane.
2. If you select it with a right click, then a menu pops up, from which you select the first item: **Add Index Entry to Selected Targets**. Alternatively,

select the file or anchor with a standard (left) click and select the **Add Index Entry** icon/button (a key) from the button bar.
3. Type in the index entry.
4. Hit <Enter>.

You will notice that the index entry you created now appears in the right Index Entry pane, replacing the automatically generated index entry for the same URL. A key icon now precedes the newly indexed entry. This icon indicates that you have created or edited the index entry.

You can easily add additional index entries for the same Web page or anchor, with the **Add Index Entry to Selected Targets** box still open.

Indexing Main Entries and Subentries

If you want to add a subentry, type it following a comma after the main entry (Figure 6.5).

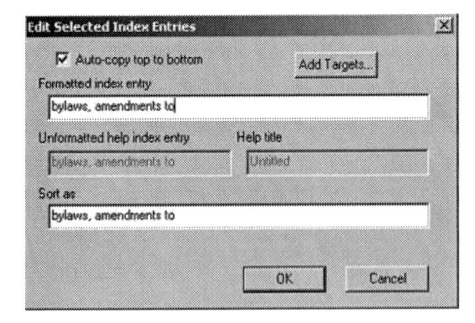

Figure 6.5

With respect to the commas, what HTML Indexer does later when you generate the index is quite clever. If, at the end of the indexing project, you have a main entry with only one subentry, then the subentry is kept as part of the main entry separated by the comma, as an inverted main entry. But, if you have two or more instances of the same main entry with different text following the comma, these will become subentries. The main entry will not be hyperlinked to any page.

If you were to type **bylaws, amendments to** and enter no more entries beginning with bylaws, in the completed index the entry will be a single hyperlinked main entry:

bylaws, amendments to

But if you were to create a second entry, such as **bylaws, officer requirements,** then the resulting index will have two hyperlinked subentries under a nonlinked main entry, as in the following example:

> bylaws
> > amendments to
> > officer requirements

If you were to enter instead a second entry of simply **bylaws** without any comma and text following, in order to have a hyperlinked main entry, then the resulting index will look like this:

> bylaws
> bylaws, amendments to

By default, HTML Indexer will not create a main entry with only a single subentry. If you wish to change this into a main entry of **bylaws** with a single subentry **amendments to**, you must edit the generated index file afterward in your HTML editing software or in Notepad, outside of HTML Indexer. If the index is large, and it's not practical to individually change each instance of a main entry with a single subentry, there are two other suggested techniques. "HTML Indexer Tips and Techniques" on the software vendor's Web site explains how to embed hyperlinking code into the index entries. According to an October 2006 article by Mike Unwalla in *The Indexer*, you can type in some special character string (such as xxx) and then use a macro afterward to remove the lines of HTML code with xxx in them.

You may also create a third level (sub-subentry) in a similar manner. Do this by typing a second comma and a sub-subentry after more than one identical main-entry/subentry pair as follows:

> main entry, subentry, first sub-subentry
> main entry, subentry, second sub-subentry

You can continue on to create fourth-level entries following this pattern, but this technique can get quite confusing both for you as the indexer and later for the user of the index.

You might, of course, want a comma in an entry to *not* be treated as a potential separator of a main entry and subentry. For example, you have a second comma within a main entry or subentry, or a comma is needed in an inverted name, such as **Last name, First Name**. To retain the comma, insert a backslash immediately preceding the comma: **Last name\, First Name**.

A backslash is also needed just before quotation marks. Figure 6.6 shows what it looks like to enter an index entry with a subentry and a backslash before a second comma.

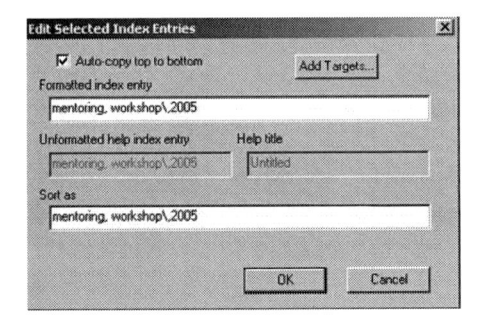

Figure 6.6

"Sort as" Field

If you want to force the alphabetical sorting of the term to deviate from the default alphabetical sort (which is word by word), you may edit the text in the Sort as field. This might be the case for the removal of definite articles or prefixes in titles or names.

Add Targets

The button for **Add Targets...** refers to the target window for the output index. This can be changed if you want to output the index to a Web page frame. Otherwise, simply ignore it.

EDITING ENTRIES AND CREATING ANCHORS
Creating Additional Entries

It is easy to create additional index entries for the same Web page or anchor, because you simply keep the **Add Index Entry to Selected Targets** box open and type in additional entries and then hit <Enter> each time you complete an entry. Because the index entry just entered is kept in the box, you can easily edit it, such as by inverting terms, to create a double post. You can even keep the **Add Index Entry to Selected Targets** box open and edit as you select different page URLs.

If you decide to go back and add an additional entry to an anchor already indexed, make sure that you select the specific anchor from the left-hand Project Tree pane and not from the right-hand Index Entry pane. Otherwise, when you add an index entry, it will automatically be appended in an identical manner to *all* the anchors within that page, rather than to only the anchor of your choice.

Deleting Entries

You will undoubtedly come across pages and especially anchors, such as **#top** for the top of the page, that should not be indexed. Simply select the index entry line in the right Index Entry pane and hit the delete key. Don't worry, it does not delete the actual file or anchor.

Editing Entries

To change an entry you have already entered, simply double-click on the entry in the right Index Entry pane, and the index entry will come up in an **Edit Selected Index Entries** box, highlighted for you to type over. This box functions essentially the same as the **Add Index Entry to Selected Targets** box. The only difference is that the box does not remain open after clicking OK, since you are not expected to create double posts here. Nevertheless, you can use the **Edit Selected Index Entries** box to create a new index entry for a URL selected from the right pane, since even the creation of new index entries can be considered "editing" the automatically generated index entries. However, if you select the index entries to add/edit from the right pane, you do not get the benefit of being able to make repeated index entry additions.

Adding Anchors

If, when viewing a Web page in your browser, you decide that an additional anchor is desired for indexing, where no anchor exists, such as at a heading level, you can easily call up that page in your HTML editor to create the anchor and then add that page back to your indexing project to complete the indexing. Here is the procedure:

1. With the file selected in the left Project Tree pane, select **Edit > Selected Source File**. The HTML editor program that you have previously specified in **Preferences > HTML Tools...** will automatically open the selected Web page file for editing.
2. Create the desired named anchor(s) within the Web page HTML file.
3. Save the revised Web page HTML file.
4. Switch back into HTML Indexer, and make sure that the edited file is still selected in the left Project Tree pane.
5. Select from the menu **Actions > Remove Selected Files and URLs from Project**. (If you accidentally remove the wrong file, just press CTRL+Z to undo.)
6. To add the file back, select **Actions > Add Files**. In the **Add Files to Project** box, browse to select the updated Web page file and click on **Add** or **<Enter>**, then **Close**.
7. Expand the folder in the left Project Tree pane to find the updated Web page file, and then expand the updated file to find the new anchors.
8. Add index entries to the new anchors.

Sorting the Index Entries for Editing

At any time you wish, you may alphabetically sort the index entries in the right pane for checking and editing. You may sort all the index entries or you may select only a single Web page to sort the index entries for that page. In the right Index Entry pane, click on the column header Index Entry in order to alphabetize by index entry. With the use of the comma separator, subentries are also alphabetically sorted for each main entry. You may also sort by index entry source type (first column) or by target file name (third column). This last type of sort is very helpful when editing your index to make sure that you have created main entries consistently.

Generating the Index File

If you want to check on how things look, you can create the output index file at any time before you finish. Simply select from the menu **Actions > Make Index** or select the **Make Index** icon/button (a key inserted into a lower case letter i) from the button bar.

Since this is a Web index, you will need to view it in your Web browser. Prior to generating the index, if you select **Preferences > HTML tools** and under **Auto-open Output Index With** click on **Browser,** the index will automatically open in your chosen browser. Make sure that the generated HTML index file is in the same folder on your computer as the Web site pages, so that the links will work.

If the resulting index does not have the subentries correctly indented, most likely the default setting for indenting needs to be changed. Go to **Preferences > Project Style Settings...** and then select the tab for **CSS**. Check the option **Use Nonbreaking Spaces**.

CROSS-REFERENCES AND EXTERNAL URLS

Creating Linked Cross-References

HTML Indexer has a function to automatically create a *See* or *See also* cross-reference that is hyperlinked from one entry to another entry. You may write the cross-reference at any time; it does not matter what, if anything, is selected in the left Project Tree pane at the time. The procedure is as follows:

1. From the main menu, select **Actions > Create Cross-Reference...** or select the **Create X-refs** icon/button from the button bar.

2. The **Create Cross-Reference** box pops up (Figure 6.7). Fill in the top left box with the entry after which the reference will follow.

3. Fill in the bottom left box with the destination of the reference, which will become hypertext.

In the **Separator** box, the default is a period. You can remove or change it to your preferences. In the **Reference Text** box, the default is *See* italicized. You can remove the HTML code for italics or change it to something else if you want. You can also change this to *See also*. When the index is created, the cross-reference will appear as follows:

    chapter bylaws. *See* <u>bylaws</u>

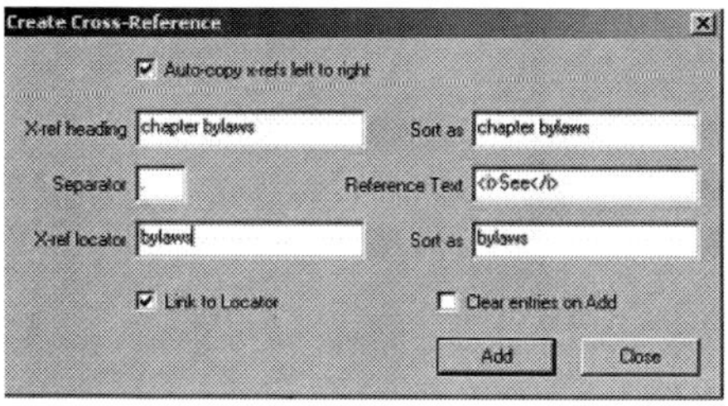

Figure 6.7

Just remember, for any cross-reference to work as an internal link, what you type into the X-ref locator field has to match *exactly* the text of an existing index entry, whether it is a main entry alone or a main entry followed by a comma and a subentry. You can copy and paste entries, by selecting an entry from the right Index Entry pane, calling up the **Edit Selected Index Entries** box, and then copying the entry from there into the appropriate field within the **Create Cross-Reference** box.

References work in either direction between main entry/subentry combinations, too. Remember, if you are referencing and linking to a subentry, the link will jump so that the referenced subentry is at the top of the user's screen view, and thus the main entry cannot be seen. You might not want this, so you might prefer to link to the main entry instead. Also, remember that if you reference and link to an entry near the end of the index, the jump link cannot display the referenced term at the top of the screen if the end of the page is reached at the bottom of the screen.

You may wish to create a cross-reference that links directly to the source text on another page of the Web site, rather than to another entry within the index. HTML Indexer's cross-reference feature supports this kind of cross-reference as well, but you must type the hyperlinking code preceding the referenced term within the **X-Ref locator field** in the **Create Cross-Reference** box. You must type the hyperlinking code in reverse, with the closing </a> tag preceding the link tag of <a href=, and you must type backslashes preceding the quotation marks. An example of how to enter the cross-reference is the following:

```
</a><a href=\"bylaws.htm\">bylaws
```

All cross-references are kept in a separate folder in the left Project Tree pane, but they will display interspersed among the index entries when alphabetized in the right Index Entry pane.

Editing "See also" References

Because *See also* references are created in HTML Indexer exactly the same way as *See* references, the result is an unlinked term with a reference to a linked term.

Since you will have already created an entry for both terms, a duplicate line will automatically be created in the index. The result will look like the following:

> executive board. *See also* <u>officers</u>
> <u>executive board</u>

This is simply how HTML Indexer works. It will not put two hypertext links on the same line. The only thing you can do is edit the index afterward in your HTML editing software or Notepad, so as to leave a single line:

> <u>executive board</u>. *See also* <u>officers</u>

If the index is large, and it's not practical to individually change each *See also* reference, as suggested by Unwalla in *The Indexer*, you could type in some codes (such as xxx) and then use a macro afterward to remove the lists of HTML code with xxx in them.

Indexing External URLs

If you want your index to include references to files that either are external to your Web site or are non-HTML files, you may incorporate them to your project through the **Add External URLs** function. To do this, you will need to copy and paste each URL. Before you begin, browse to the desired Web page or file in your Web browser:

1. In your browser, copy the entire URL from the URL bar.
2. In HTML Indexer, from the menu select **Actions > Add External URLs...** or select the **Add External URLs** icon/button from the button menu.
3. In the **Add External URLs to Project** box that pops up, paste the copied URL from your clipboard.
4. Click on the **Add** button or hit **<Enter>** to add the URL.
5. Repeat for each URL.

The URL has now been added to the External URLs folder of the left Project Tree pane and can also be viewed in the right Index Entry pane. The **Add External URLs to Project** box remains open with the URL in the field highlighted so that you can either edit it or paste over a new URL in order to index successive external URLs. As explained previously, you may add the URLs of non-HTML files that are part of the Web site in the same manner.

After you have added the URLs for external links or non-HTML files, in the left Project Tree pane expand the folder called **External URLs** to see the individual URLs for indexing.

HTML Indexer for Creating Web Indexes 93

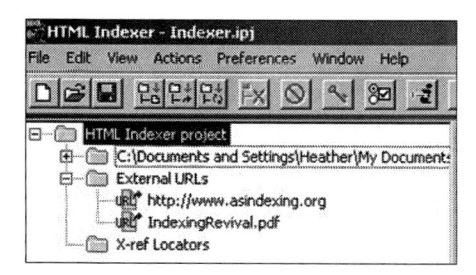

Figure 6.8

In the example shown in Figure 6.8, you can see to the left of the Project Tree pane the addition of one external link with a complete Web URL and one PDF file.

Select each URL link and add index entries in the same way as it was done with the Web pages.

PROJECT STYLE SETTINGS

From the **Preferences** menu, you may choose among numerous index style preferences either as a default for all of your index projects or specifically for a current index project.

Under both menu options, **Project Style Settings...** and **Default Style Settings...**, the style setting options are the same, divided into six tabbed groups.

You may set the **Project Style Settings** first and then select **Save Project Styles as Default**, or you may set the **Default Style Setting** first and then select **Apply Default Styles to Project**.

Following is a brief description of the six tabbed groups of settings (with a screenshot, Figure 6.9, of only the first one).

1. Links to Headings

Links to Headings (Figure 6.9) refers to the "ribbon" of the letters of the alphabet, which appears typically at the top of the index. The options are the following:

- Text or graphic letters (if you already have files for the graphics).
- Whether or not to have vertical bars between the letters.
- Placement of the list of letters at the top of the page only, the top and the bottom of the page, or in a separate frame.
- Whether to include symbols and numbers (if the index has entries beginning with them) at the start of the list of letters.
- Whether to have a horizontal rule to separate the letters from the index.

[Figure 6.9: Project Style Settings dialog — Links to Headings tab]

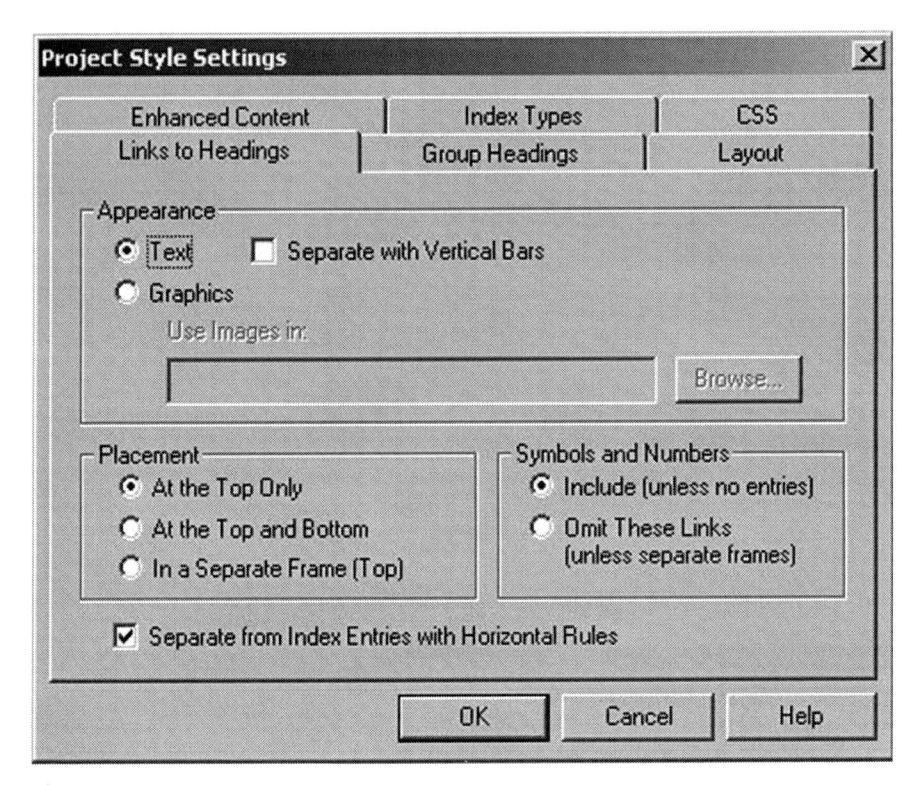

Figure 6.9

2. Group Headings

Group Headings also refers to the ribbon list of the letters of the alphabet. The additional option here is how to handle letters of the alphabet for which there are no index entries. The options are the following:

- Grouping the letter(s) for which there are no entries with the previous letter that does have entries to create a range. For example, with no entries for the letter Q, the heading letters display as **P–Q**.
- Grouping the letter(s) without entries with the next letter that does have entries to create a range. For with no entries for the letter Q, the heading letters display as **Q–R**.
- Omitting the letters for which there are no index entries. For example, with no entries for the letter Q, the heading letters display as **P R**.

3. Layout

Layout refers to the basic layout of the index. The options are the following:

- Naming the index page title, that is, what goes in-between the <t> and </t> tags and appears in the title bar of the Web site visitor's browser.
- Naming the index page heading, that is, what text appears at the top of the index (which may be the same as the page title).
- Making subentries appear in hanging-indented format (the common format) or in run-in format. The run-in format, which is commonly preferred in scholarly books, can also be used in Web indexing, particularly in the case of online periodical indexes where there might be a long series of "subentries" indicating issue date and/or number and volume.
- Putting the index into one, two, or three columns and allowing long lines to wrap.

At the bottom is also an option to check "Put Groups in Separate Files," which creates a separate Web page for each letter of the alphabet or range of letters. This presentation may be desirable if the index becomes very long.

4. Enhanced Content

This Enhanced Content tab includes two options. One is to indicate a specified HTML file to be used as a frame for either the top or bottom content of the index page, so that the index pages fits in with the same graphic design as other pages on the Web site.

The other option on this tab is to indicate preferences with respect to the "Return to top" links within the page: whether to have them, what the text should be if not "Return to top," or whether to use a graphic file (which you must name Return.gif) instead. You might choose to incorporate hyperlinked graphic up-arrows instead of using the text "Return to top."

5. Index Types

For the generated index file, the default is HTML with the extension of .htm. The other options are HTML Help (.hhk) and JavaHelp (.xml). You would generate indexes of the latter two types if you were creating an index for online help documentation that exists in one of these formats. The procedure for creating indexes for online help is a topic beyond the scope of this book.

6. CSS

Under this tab, the choice is between two methods of indenting subentries. CSS, which stands for cascading style sheets, is used to specify styles that can be kept in a separate file.

If you are not using an external style sheet, then you need to change the default to **Use Nonbreaking Spaces**. With this choice, subentries are indented by the automatic insertion of five nonbreaking spaces with the code of: **   **.

If you are using an external style sheet, then the selection should be **Use Classes**, but you also need to specify the file name of the external style sheet. You can use a style sheet, even if you don't know anything about creating style sheets. The HTML Indexer package comes with a default style sheet file, which you may use as-is or alter if you are comfortable with CSS. The file is called **Indexer.css** and resides in your HTML Indexer folder. However, you cannot use it within that folder. You must first copy the file into the folder of your Web site index where it will be accessible when the Web site and its index are uploaded.

Also under the CSS tab is the option to type in any attributes you want to include in the <BODY> tag that will be included in the style sheet. These can include font style and size, background, use of headings, and so forth.

MODIFICATIONS OF INDEXED FILES

Unlike other Web indexing tools, HTML Indexer modifies all the indexed Web pages as part of its method for self-maintaining the index. It actually stores the index entries on the page indexed, by inserting them in a comment block in the HEAD section of the indexed page. Visitors to the Web site index do not see this data in their browser. It starts out like this:

```
<!— HTML Indexer V4.0 - Do not edit this comment block.
     Target="#"
          IndexAs=
```

There is also a corresponding comment block within the HEAD section at the top of the index page(s). This data ensures that HTML Indexer won't create an index entry that points to a nonexistent target.

For a contract indexer working on someone else's Web site, it can be inconvenient to have to keep the actual content files until they are indexed and return them modified to the client. The client may want to make modifications on the site in the meantime. Some clients may also not like the idea of having to upload the site again with files modified by someone else. If, however, you are responsible for continued updating and maintenance of the Web site, then I advise republishing the index-linked pages.

An index created in HTML Indexer without re-uploading the files with the comments of index entries will still function; however, it does not have that extra security/guarantee that the index entries will always work. Yet this is no worse than an index created in any other method. The imbedding of the comment code is merely an added feature than you may or may not choose to take advantage of. The developer of HTML Indexer, however, considers ease of maintenance and guaranteed accuracy as the greatest strengths of HTML Indexer.

CONCLUSION

HTML Indexer offers several advantages over XRefHT: (1) the ease with which you can add multiple index entries to the same Web page or anchor, (2) a simpler method to add cross-references, (3) an efficient method to add additional anchors to a Web page manually and add the page data back into the index file, and (4) a feature for automatically maintaining the index. Its main drawback is the lack of a spell checker and of any find/replace feature. According to the developer (in an e-mail message of November 27, 2006), there are no plans to add a spell checker or other major enhancements, although minor updates can still be expected.

FURTHER READING

"HTML Indexer Tips and Techniques." finitesite.com/infor/Tips.htm

Unwalla, Mike. "Web Indexing: Extending the Functionality of HTML Indexer." *The Indexer*, Vol. 25, No. 2, October 2006.

SOFTWARE RESOURCES

HTML Indexer, www.html-indexer.com

Chapter 7

Web Site Indexing Techniques

Now that we have covered the technical aspects of how to index Web sites, this chapter presents methods and techniques for writing the indexes of Web sites regardless of the software used. Even if you are already an experienced indexer of books or periodicals, you will find issues peculiar to the indexing of Web sites in the approach to indexing, the selection of which pages and topics to index, and in the creation of cross-references. How to word the entries and when to create subentries will be covered in Chapter 8.

APPROACH TO WEB SITE INDEXING

The mental process of Web site indexing has more in common with periodical or encyclopedia indexing than with back-of-the-book indexing. Instead of finding a concept and indexing it with locators pointing to a range of pages, you start with the Web page or subsection, like a periodical or newspaper article, determine its main topics, and index all of those concepts with the locator of that page or heading/anchor. Personally, I find this kind of indexing a little easier than book indexing. You only need to focus on one Web page at a time, without worrying whether a concept carries over for several pages. Furthermore, while book indexing requires you to read every word, in periodical or Web site indexing you can often skim the headings to get the substance of the page.

Getting an Overview

When preparing to index a book, the indexer can use various techniques to grasp the potentially recurring index entries and begin to envision the structure of the index. For example, you might read the table of contents and skim the subchapter level breakdowns within the chapters. Web sites, although lacking a traditional table of contents, provide a rough equivalent in the site map. When a site map is available, it is a good idea to look at it before starting to index. Many sites, however, do not contain site maps. Whether or not there is a site map, another way to get an idea of the scope of a Web site involves looking at the navigation menu. If the menu has a secondary or tertiary level to the menu, you then should examine each level of the menu.

Understanding the Audience

As in all indexing, indexers need to know their audience in order to choose the right terms. For an intranet, the audience is clearly the organization's employees. For a Web site, its very location on the World Wide Web means that it will interface with a diverse audience. By asking the Web site owner and/or by exploring the contents of the Web site, the indexer can learn the various kinds of potential users of the Web site. For a corporate Web site, this includes current customers, potential customers, potential employees, competitors doing research, market researchers, potential vendors, and possibly even investors and potential investors. With this insight, the indexer then knows which terms to choose so that all these types of visitors to the Web site will be accommodated.

Order of Page Indexing

When indexing printed materials, the natural flow begins from page 1 and proceeds in page order. On Web sites, no numeric page order exists, although there is often a hierarchical structure. The indexer does not need to try to index the pages in structural order. Unlike in print indexing where a topic may continue from one page to the next and necessitate a page range locator (for example, 37–39), Web pages are fluid in length, allowing a specific topic of discussion to remain on one page. A broader topic might require several pages, but there would probably be a page higher up in the hierarchy from which these multiple pages are linked, and it is to this intermediate page that the index entry can point.

Since you do not have a page number to mark how far you have progressed with the project, you need to come up with your own tracking method. The simplest way to organize the project is to index the pages in whatever order they appear in your list, whether in the Windows Explorer folder and file directory or the list that appears when you open up the Web site folder in an indexing tool such as XRefHT or HTML Indexer. Typically, the pages will appear within each subfolder in alphabetical order by page title. This might not seem a practical order in which to read the Web pages for indexing, but since specific topics are kept to one page, this is not as bad as it sounds. Furthermore, the subfolders will have the pages grouped to some degree by topic, and that is the best approach—to index by topic cluster. Alternatively, you could browse the downloaded Web site from its home page and do a first pass of the pages within the top level of the hierarchy/navigational menu, thus getting an overview of the range of topics. Trying to access all the pages via the site's own navigational menu, however, can be confusing, because it's easy to lose your place, so I recommend indexing the rest of the pages in the order in which they appear on your file list.

Finding the Anchors

In dealing with Web sites, you are not just creating entries for the topics at the page level, rather you are indexing to the point of named anchors within pages, if appropriate. When you view a Web page in your browser, however, the named anchors do not appear there. Sometimes you know the anchors are there (for example, when a list of hypertext headings appears near the top of a page, and when clicked on, jump down to headings below on the page). But other times you find no indication of named anchors for potential use in indexing.

The indexing tools XRefHT and HTML Indexer both retrieve named anchors for you. If you are not using these tools, however, then you must proceed to find the anchors by searching for them in the code view of your Web browser. After selecting **View > Source** in your browser, you perform a **Find** in the code view on the start of the anchor code: **<a name=**. This procedure becomes quite tedious, and you are likely to retrieve unnecessary anchors, such as "top of page." It is also easy to lose your way in the code. What I recommend, instead of searching on all anchors in the code, is to first identify the section headings in the normal browser view, select the heading, and then perform a search on the heading text in the code view. When you find the text, check to see if there is the code for an anchor immediately preceding the heading. Anchor names are not always intuitive, because they are restricted to one word.

Viewing Web Pages

When indexing Web pages, no matter what tools you use, you will need to switch back and forth between your indexing program and the actual Web pages that you are reading. You can switch screens, or tile the two programs on a large monitor or even use two monitors. I find switching screens sufficient.

For those who are accustomed to marking their printed pages prior to keying the entries in an indexing program, you have to get used to doing it differently. I do not recommend printing out Web pages. The graphics take up too much time and ink/toner to print, and a single Web page may consume numerous pieces of paper. On a positive note, you can scan Web pages relatively easily on screen. After all, they are designed to be read online. The best designs keep paragraphs short and insert lots of headings to break up the content.

Creating Additional Anchors

An additional step to Web site indexing is the creation of more named anchors in the Web pages where none exist and for which it is desirable to have an entry link. These anchors would likely be needed for headings at the start of sections comprising one or more paragraphs within a rather long, scrollable Web page. If the page is so short that no scrollbar appears, no anchors are needed.

If you are responsible for updating the Web pages yourself, creating additional anchors will not be a problem. If, however, you are an offsite contractor (i.e., freelance indexer) who has downloaded the site or received the site files on a CD and thus are not working on the live site, an agreement on how anchors should be added needs to be reached before the indexing begins. Either you will add the anchors to the Web pages and send the revised Web pages back, or you will write up a list of anchors, their names, and where they are to be added for the Web site owner to insert.

CHOOSING WHICH PAGES TO INDEX

When deciding which pages to index, you should first consider the size and structure of the site. If it is very large, you need to agree with the site owner what to include. Certain sections might be omitted, or the index might cover only a section of the site, such as only an intranet or only an extranet portion, or only the pages of the top levels of the site. Within the defined section of the Web site, there are still other considerations in choosing which pages to include. Do not assume that all Web pages should be indexed.

Home Page

If there is a home page link on every page of the Web site, including the index page, then you do not need an index entry for "home page." If, however, there is no home page link from the index page and from most pages of the Web site (an ill-advised design), then an entry for "home page" would be helpful in the index.

Additional index terms are probably not needed. Most of the information on the home page tends to be repeated elsewhere in the site in more detail. The home page merely presents the overall navigation, provides a brief introduction as well as some illustrations. If, however, the home page includes additional, specific indexable information and that information resides only on the home page, then this content could be referenced with the appropriate term(s).

Site Map and Site Index Pages

Similarly, if the site map, a site search, or other general navigation or search features are available in a menu or buttons on most pages of the Web site, or at least from the page with the A–Z index, you do not need to add them in the index. If a site map or a site search feature is not available from most pages of a Web site and also not available from the menu on the index page, then include it in the index.

You might expect that since the site map acts like a table of contents and since a book index does not include a table of contents as an index entry, then the site map should be excluded from the Web site index. However, unlike in a book where the user always knows to find the table of contents at the front, the site map in a Web site does not have a standard location. Ideally, though, the site map and any other search features are available on the menu of every page of the Web site.

An index entry for the index page is, of course, unnecessary, but I have actually seen this in a Web site index created by an inexperienced indexer: **Index (this page)**.

Navigation Pages

There is no need to index "navigation" pages. These are Web pages that introduce a section of the Web site and give brief descriptions and links to the pages below them in the hierarchy. The purpose of these "intermediate" pages is to help with navigation, especially if a site has multiple levels of hierarchy but lacks a multi-level navigation menu (dropdown menus). When using an index, the Web site visitor skips any navigation page. Therefore, a link to it is not needed.

An example of a navigation page that you would probably not index is the Services page of the Gleason Public Library (www.gleasonlibrary.org) site shown in Figure 7.1. The paragraph of text merely summarizes the pages in the section.

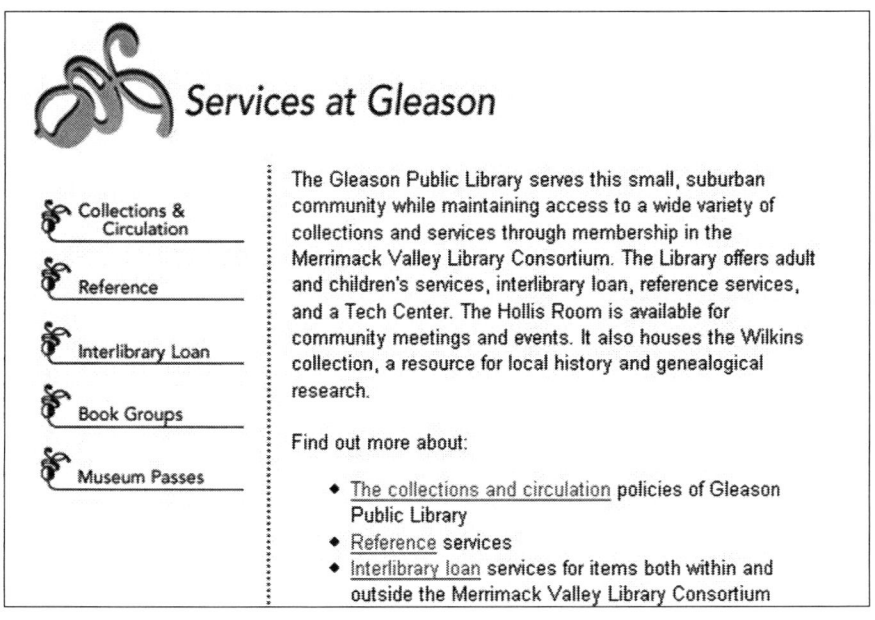

Figure 7.1

Not all types of navigation pages should be excluded from an index, though. Include the page if it provides a lengthy list of resources, such as a product list or list of articles, from which the user may want to make multiple choices and thus return to in order to choose more.

Function Pages

A site may also have pages with minimal content but instead contain a box or a form for the user to fill in, such as a feedback or comments form. You might be tempted to skip such a page in indexing, because it lacks significant text content. On the contrary, such a page should be indexed. Unlike print material, a Web site serves not merely to inform the user but may also permit the user to perform certain functions. The user will want to find the desired Web page in order to utilize a function.

Dynamically Generated Pages

In a dynamic Web site, with a searchable database or interactive forms, some pages are called up as part of the dynamic function of the site. An example is a page that merely confirms a user's input. These pages cannot be reached from the navigation menu, but as you go through all the pages of the Web site to index, you will come across them. An example is the from-process page from the Web Indexing SIG site, which depending on what the user entered, might look like the screen shown in Figure 7.2.

Figure 7.2

Do not index these pages. If you view such a page in your Web browser, you might see nothing or almost nothing in your WYSIWYG view, but you will find some code in the code view.

Frames

A Web "page" for a header or margin frame should also be excluded from the index. All frames appear individually as regular Web pages with the .htm or .html extension in your list of files to index, but once you view the file in your browser, you will notice that it is merely a frame. A site with frames would likely have only one, two, or three of these header, margin, or footer frames that would be skipped in the indexing. Other pages as the main frames should be indexed as appropriate.

PDF and Other Non-HTML Pages

Pages of a Web site that are in portable document format (PDF) and with file names that end in the .pdf extension should be indexed along with the HTML pages. They are an integral part of the Web site, accessed from the site pages, and accessed with the Web browser. It might help the user, however, to indicate parenthetically or with a graphic icon in the index that the page is PDF format, since the page requires PDF reader software to open, and will take longer to load. An example of an index entry indicating PDF format is on the Web Indexing SIG Web site index:

> usability of Web indexes (Kingsley presentation, pdf)

Other documents in a Web site, such as Word or Excel files, are less likely indexed as part of the Web site, because they cannot be viewed through a Web browser and thus are not necessarily considered part of the site. When these files are accessed through the Web site, instead of being viewed, the user is prompted to download the file. If these files are chosen to be indexed, the indexer should indicate the file format and that the link is for a download.

CHOOSING WHICH HEADINGS TO INDEX

Now that we have determined which pages to index, we move on to determine whether to index specific sections within a page. When deciding what to index within the pages chosen, you should first consider content as grouped by sections and headings, where an anchor may or may not already be present. You also need to consider simply what is worth indexing. Section headings, as we are defining them for indexing, do not necessarily have the heading HTML tags. Section headings may merely display in bold or a larger font, or they might even be a graphic.

Section headings occur more frequently in Web content than in printed documents, because they facilitate onscreen reading. Thus, section headings on a Web page may be spaced apart as little as every two or three lines, whereas in a printed manual they might occur after several paragraphs, and in a book they might appear only on every two or three pages. Therefore, just because each new paragraph has a heading does not mean that each paragraph should be indexed individually.

When a user jumps from an index entry to an anchor at a heading within a Web page, it is very likely that the user will also scroll a little both up and down to get some context for the topic and see any information nearby. For this reason, too, it is not necessary to index to every paragraph or frequently occurring section heading, but rather to group a few paragraphs or sections together if they cover the same broader subject.

When deciding whether to index at a section heading, consider the following issues:

1. **Whether there is a significant amount of information**
   Sometimes there is as little as a sentence or two under a heading. Such a heading does not usually merit indexing.

2. **Whether information is too detailed, trivial, or off-topic for the site**
   This may happen with information under especially frequent section headings or for sections within articles. For example, a Web site of a

professional association may contain a page on the association history with sections for each decade. Indexing each decade would be too detailed and trivial for the broader theme of the Web site.

3. **Whether content within a section has a special focus and audience**
Different users have different interests in mind and might want to look up different sections. But if all the users are likely to want to read the entire larger section or page, there is less of a need for indexing individual subsections. For example, a Web site of an organization has a page on its "Mission and Vision" with a short section on each. The same users are probably interested in both the Mission and the Vision and not either in isolation, so it better meets their needs to index them together, as "mission and vision" and "vision and mission." On the other hand, a page on membership may have sections for regular membership and institutional membership. Since these two topics are aimed at different users, it's best to index these two headings individually.

4. **Whether the content of a section is unique to the site**
Although information usually does not repeat within a Web site, sometimes general "about us" information appears in more than one page to fill space. Extra indexing is not needed for the same information in multiple places.

5. **Whether the heading is near the bottom of the page**
When the page is short or you have already scrolled to the bottom, links to anchors cannot display the anchored heading at the top of the screen as the user might expect. If there is more than one section near the bottom of the page, an index to the lower section will retrieve the Web page with the upper section also displaying, which could be confusing to the user. The bottom sections may need to be indexed together under a commonly shared broader topic. If a Web page is very short (i.e., can fit onto one screen), but has multiple headings in it, there is no need to add an anchor at a heading, because the complete Web page will display in the browser the same way, whether the anchor is "jumped to" or not. The browser window cannot "jump down" if the bottom of the page is already displayed. This is not to say that the topics themselves should not be used as index terms, but rather that the index terms should not link to anchors too close to the bottom of the page.

6. **Whether the heading topics are of interest beyond the scope of the page**
If all the heading topics are found only on a single page, and it is obvious that they are to be found only on that page, then there is less of a reason to index the headings individually. For example, if a Web site of an organization has a page listing branch facilities by specialty and another page listing facilities by location, it makes more sense to index the specific headings for facility specialization than to index the specific headings for geographic location. Visitors to the site are likely to look up subjects of specialties in the index, but they are

not likely to look up cities or states in the index. If they are interested in geographic locations, they can look up "locations" in the index, and that page will provide the information they seek. There is little interest in geographic topics beyond the scope of the page on facilities locations.

7. **Whether the headings are within article-type documents**
If a site contains articles and those articles have headings within them, typically we don't index to that level of detail. The articles are reference just at the overall article level. For example, an organization Web site, such as that for the Web Indexing SIG, might have a few articles on it, and the articles have headings in them to facilitate reading. Since the index focuses on the site overall and not the detailed content of the articles, indexing to specific topics within the articles is probably not necessary and might even confuse the user. More specifically, headings within articles should not be indexed for the following reasons:

- The headings may not make sense out of context.
- Users don't like to be tossed into the middle of an article, but rather need the context of the entire article.
- Users do not expect such in-depth indexing from a site index.
- If the article is long, it should have jump links to headings from hypertext contents at the top of the page of the article.

8. **Whether there are anchors at the headings already**
If the site has been in existence for some time with an anchor at a section, repeat visitors might already be accustomed to jumping to the section from elsewhere on the page or the Web site. Therefore, they might expect to find the section referenced in the index. The presence of anchors also indicates the section's importance from the point of view of the Web site creator/owner. Finally, of course, it makes your job easier if there are anchors already. This should be the least important factor in deciding whether to index at a heading, but it is still a consideration.

CHOOSING WHAT TOPICS TO INDEX

When indexing, you need to assume the point of view of the index user. When you look at the text of a page to be indexed, consider the following questions:

- Is there a topic here that someone will want to look up?
- Is there significant information on the topic? Is there something about it beyond a mere mention of the term?
- Will the user appreciate being brought to this page or anchor location within the page when looking up the term, rather than being annoyed at finding only insufficient or trivial information?

One of the most common mistakes of beginning indexers is to over-index, that is, to pick up references to pages where there really is not enough significant information on the topic. Trivial information should not be indexed. Over-indexing is actually not as likely in Web site indexing as in book indexing, because Web sites tend to be written more concisely than books, and include less anecdotal information. Still, the indexer should be on guard not to index everything just because it is there.

Indexing Web sites typically does not require the depth of indexing expected for books. Book indexes tend to be more exhaustive and specific, requiring a more thorough analysis of the text. Before adding more topics to an index, stop to consider the context of the page and the site. A topic may seem appropriate to index within the context of the Web page, but not within the context of the entire site. On the other hand, if the topic is likely to occur on more than one page within the site, it becomes a better candidate for indexing.

Although in general I am talking about indexing text, graphics may also be indexed if they provide important information. Maps, charts, graphs, diagrams, etc., should probably be covered in the index. Individual photos, however, rarely provide information for indexing. A page of photos may be indexed with a single term "**photos of...**" but individual photos do not need indexing, unless the site serves as an archive or database of images.

Indexing Beyond Headings

While section headings provide a logical point of indexing, you should not rely on headings alone as a source of index terms. There could be more than one idea to be indexed within a section under a heading, the headings could be imprecise, or there might be no headings. You also need to consider named entities (proper nouns), in addition to subjects, for indexing.

More Than One Idea in a Section

Quite often a section of text may have multiple topics for the index. While it is tempting for the sake of speed to read headings only, it is important to scan the text, too, to look for other indexable concepts.

Imprecise Headings

Headings or titles, especially in an article-type document, might be worded to fit in with the flow of the document, more than to indicate the main point to be indexed. In Web pages, designers use headings frequently to break up the text to make it easier to read on screen, and thus headings are not always used to group information of a single topic. Such headings might have arbitrary names. Examples of imprecise headings are those within the article page "Sitemaps and Site Indexes: What They Are and Why You Should Have Them," which include **Can you see it?**, **It's as easy as A-B-C**, **But how do I choose?**, **Location matters**, and **Making it easy on yourself**. Don't even try to turn headings such as these into index entries.

No Headings

Many Web pages, especially shorter ones, have no headings at all. These pages should be indexed as appropriate for the content of the text. Ironically, it's more work sometimes to index a shorter page than a longer one!

Indexing Named Entities

Names of people, organizations, departments, products, programs, and so on, should be integrated into an index of topics. While some books maintain separate name and subject indexes, these divided indexes are not as prominent in Web sites. Web site indexes contain very few personal names; many more proper nouns are based on departmental or program names. It is not always obvious to the user, though, how to distinguish such department and program names from topical terms, so it is best to keep all terms in a single index. Some site "indexes" consist solely of proper nouns, such as departments, but this is more accurately called a directory, rather than an index.

Personal Names

Index personal names minimally on Web sites. People's titles and roles change frequently, so names in an index could require frequent updates. Rather than indexing the names of the current officers of an organization, it is preferable to index merely the titles and the offices. Historical names, however, such as an organization's past officers or founders, can safely be indexed, and you should include them if sufficient information is present.

Organization or Department Names

When sufficient information is provided in the text, it is important to index organization names, including variant short forms and acronyms. It's generally not a good idea, though, to include in an index of an organization's Web site the name of the organization itself, because it would appear too many times in the index. An exception is for the most general information in an "About Us" type of page.

Events and Awards

Do not index current and upcoming events or awards listed on a Web site, since they change frequently. On the other hand, you may index names of recurring events and awards for which historical or general undated information appears. These could include names of conferences, trade shows, competitions, fairs, festivals, holidays, or seasons. Index common events, such as holidays or seasons, within longer terms reflecting the context of the Web site, such as **Winter holidays concert, Memorial Day luncheon,** or **Independence Day parade.**

Place Names

You may index geographic names, but the terms, like seasons or holidays, should relate to the context of the Web site, such as **European operations** or **New York office**, rather than simply "Europe" or "New York." As stated earlier, though, if all geographic locations mentioned in a Web reside on a single Web page, you could omit the specific locations from the index.

Considering Additional Topics

As indexers know, textual analysis is the main approach to creating an index. For Web indexing, it is also helpful to take into account the perspective of the entire Web site. Ask yourself, "What would I expect or hope to find in the index for this site?" This step can come either before or after indexing all of the pages.

If possible, look at the Web site indexes of similar types of organizations, just as you would look at a book index of an already published book on the same subject. For example, if you are indexing the Web site of a museum, look at the Web site indexes of other museums. Site indexes of various kinds of Web sites are listed on the page of Web Site Index Examples (www.web-indexing.org/web-index-examples.htm) of the Web Indexing Special Interest Group site for your reference.

This comparative approach does not work well for intranet indexing, though, since intranets are not publicly available. Nevertheless, some membership organizations and educational institutions include publicly accessible pages that are meant to serve their own members and are "intranet-like," and these are worth examining when you are indexing an intranet. On the other hand, indexers of intranets, unlike indexers of public Web sites, have the advantage of being able to directly ask the site's users for input. Stakeholders, however, may try to influence an index more than you, the indexer, would like. Ideally the creation of the index should be the indexer's decision, and it would probably be better to solicit suggestions for additional topics only after you have a final index. The users can "beta-test" the index and provide feedback.

You should also look at the index from the perspective of a user and see if certain topics that might be expected for this site are missing. For example, I created an index for a public library Web site, and only later when I pointed out the site to out-of-town users did I realize that the topic of "parking" might come up. In such cases, you may end up indexing some smaller chunks of text. But if there is at least sufficient information to satisfy the user, then the index needs to make that connection.

CREATING CROSS-REFERENCES

Cross-references provide instructions to the index user to look further in some other part of the index. Cross-references can be at the level of either a main entry or a subentry. There are two basic kinds of cross-references: *See* and *See also*. In Web site indexes, the cross-references are hyperlinked, either to a referring term within the index or directly to the source text.

Does a Web site index need to have cross-references? Yes, there will be some places in any index where a cross-reference improves the utility. So do not avoid adding them. Even if you add only one or two cross-references, the users and the Web site owner will notice them, appreciate them, and will likely be impressed that such additional thought and consideration went into creating the index.

See References

A *See* reference guides the user from a non-preferred variant to the preferred term. In a print index, the locators (page numbers) are listed at the preferred or target term only, not at the non-preferred, cross-referencing term. In Web indexes, the target term following the word *See* is hypertext, and the term before it is not hypertext. In the following example, the underlined text would be hypertext:

> non-preferred term. *See* preferred term

See references are used in printed indexes, as an alternative to "double posting" (variant entries that point to the same location), typically when synonymous main entries have subentries, to avoid wasting space by not having all the subentries repeated under each variant term. On Web sites, with undefined page lengths, there is little concern for using up space as a consequence of repeated multiple subentries. Therefore, the *See* cross-reference is not always used for this purpose in Web site indexes, and equivalent variants, even with many subentries, tend to be entered. For example, both **automobiles** and **cars** are listed along with their numerous identical subentries and identical links on the index of *Consumer Reports*, rather than having one of the two terms point as a cross-reference to the other. Even when space is not an issue, though, some indexers might not like the style of numerous duplicated entries in an index and therefore create a *See* reference instead.

Because the cross-reference term is hypertext, the destination of the link does not necessarily have to be another term within the index, but could instead be the Web page referenced by the term. This opens up another possible use for the *See* reference, which is to inform the user of the preferred term. Instead of jumping to another term in the index, the reference can name what the preferred term is while simultaneously linking directly to the page with the content, saving the user an extra click through the index. This works best when there are no subentries under the term. In fact, in Web site indexes, *See* cross-references tend to be used more often for this purpose: between main entries, without subentries, for the purpose of instructing the user as the preferred, correct term. This may especially be the case in intranets, where the correct names of departments, teams, or projects is considered important.

A well-designed index employs a combination of intra-index and direct-to-page links as appropriate for the *See* references. In the index of American Association for Artificial Intelligence: AI Topics (www.aaai.org/AITopics/html/a2z.html), under E, you will see both kinds of links under Espionage:

- Espionage, see:
  -- Military
  -- Surveillance

For one referenced term, **Military**, with no subentries, the link goes directly to the source text. For the second referenced term, **Surveillance**, which has subentries, the link is to the term within the index, so that you see the subentries.

Even if there are a few subentries under a main entry that has a cross-reference to a preferred term, the subentries could be repeated under each main entry. Table 7.1 may also be used as a guide in determining how best to create and link *See* references.

You may also have the situation where one term is preferred and there are multiple subentries, which would call for a cross-reference linked to the preferred term within the index, yet the main entry also is linked directly to the text. In this case, you might choose to do both: have the main entry linked directly to the text (rather than to another term in the index, thus saving the user a click), but also have a link to the preferred term where the subentries are located. In this case, when both terms preceding and following the cross-reference are linked, then the *See also* reference should be used, and in this case it would be *See also under*. The following example illustrates this case:

>heart disease
>   *See also under* cardiovascular disease

The preferred term is cardiovascular disease. Under that term in the index appear several subentries. The term cardiovascular disease is also linked to a general page on the topic. Therefore, the term heart disease also links to that general page on cardiovascular disease.

See also References

See also cross-references are used in a similar manner in both printed and Web indexes to guide users to related terms. Both terms in a pair are preferred, and both terms have links. The *See also* link is reciprocal and thus usually present under both terms of a relationship pair.

The Web site index of the *New South Wales Public Health Bulletin* (www.health.nsw.gov.au/public-health/phb/subject_index_for_2002Web.htm) makes extensive use of *See also* references. The following three examples are taken from that index.

Table 7.1

Main Entries	Subentries		
	None	**Few**	**Many**
Terms are equal	No cross-references; repeat terms	No cross-references; repeat terms	Perhaps cross-references linked to a chosen preferred term
One term is preferred	Cross-references linked to text	Cross-references linked to preferred term	Cross-references linked to preferred term

See also cross-references may be used to indicate closely related terms that have significant overlap in meaning or scope, or between a pair of broader and narrower terms. An example is:

<u>adolescents</u> *see also* <u>children</u>
<u>children</u> *see also* <u>adolescents</u>

Although less common, it is possible to have a *See also* reference between one term and multiple other terms, a shown in the following example:

data collection
see also <u>health status</u>; <u>notifications</u>; <u>population data</u>; <u>statistics</u>; <u>surveys</u>

Not all the cross-references, however, are reciprocal in this example. The terms **notifications**, **population data**, and **statistics** also have *See also* references pointing back to **data collection**, but the term **health status** does not.

A *See also* cross-reference may not need a link if it is pointing to a class of terms, rather than to a specific term, in what is known as a generic cross-reference. In the following example, the phrase "specific diseases" is not hyperlinked, and the italics style indicates that the phrase *specific diseases* itself is not a term in the index.

<u>bloodborne diseases</u>
see also specific diseases

See also references, like the *See* references, may link either to the referenced term within the index or directly to the source text, depending on the presence of subentries under the referenced term. For example, in the Pierce College site index (www.pierce.ctc.edu/other/siteindex.php3#A), you will find:

> Admissions
> *see also* Registration

Here, the hyperlink of the term **Registration** jumps directly to the Web page source text on Registration, rather than to the term **Registration** in the index. The cross-reference is nevertheless reciprocal, so you will find in the index under R:

> Registration
> *see also* Admissions

Here the hyperlink of the term **Admissions** jumps directly to the Web page source text on Admissions, rather than to the term **Admissions** in the index.

In either case, whether the cross-referenced term links to a target term within the index or directly to the source text, when a *See also* reference is used, the source text should be different for each of the terms of the reference. In other words, the distinct terms link to distinct pages of content, each with its own separate URL.

It's a judgment call for the indexer when to use *See also* references. The type of index and the audience are important factors. If the Web index is of the type that is also seen in print, such as a periodical index or book-type document, then users are more likely to expect cross-references and won't mind bouncing around the index a bit before getting to the source text. These indexes, therefore, can have a more liberal use of *See also* cross-references. A general index of a complete Web site, where A–Z indexes are not yet as common, should probably not have too many cross-references. If you are able to survey the site's users, this is a question to ask them. In any case, beginner indexers need to be careful not to create excessive *See also* references. While some are helpful, too many such references become distracting and complicate an index.

Cross-Reference Style

The style of the cross-references *See* and *See also* can take various forms:

- Initial capitalization or lower case
- Italics or bold, or neither or both
- A different color
- Immediately following a term or on a separate line
- If immediately following a term, whether there is punctuation, and if so, whether a period or a comma
- In parentheses or not

These style options are up to you or the Web site owner. What is important is to be consistent for all cross-references. In book publishing, the style will be dictated by the publisher. Depending on the indexing software you use, you may be able to control some of these formatting features ahead of time, rather than manually editing the generated index. In HTML Indexer you may set various style preferences. In XRefHT, you can only control on what line the cross-reference falls.

FURTHER READING

See the bibliography at the end of Chapter 8 for a list of books on indexing techniques in general that would apply to book as well as Web site indexing.

Chapter 8

Web Site Index Style and Format

The remaining topics in creating Web site indexes concern entry style and index format. The first half of this chapter discusses style issues, including the wording of the index entries and the creation of subentries. The second half takes up Web site index format, which includes the choices of heading letters, columns, top-of-page links, case of entries, indicators of special pages, and methods of indenting subentries.

WORDING OF INDEX ENTRIES

Once you have decided what to index, you next have to decide exactly how to word the entries and whether to create double posting. This is the most creative part of indexing. If you are already an experienced book indexer, this will come easily to you, but you still need to consider the particular needs of Web site indexing. Writing appropriate index entries raises issues of term length, choice of the first word of the phrase, term clarity and context, the grammatical form of the term, and the creation of subentries and possibly sub-subentries. Editing the index as a whole, the final step, provides yet another opportunity to improve wording and structure.

Length of Entries

In printed indexes, the typical design tends to use two columns to save space, making long entries clumsy. Long text has to wrap to the next line and be indented. Users may confuse these wraps with the indented subentries. Therefore, book indexers try to be as concise as possible in drafting entries. Web site indexes, on the other hand, tend to display in a single column, so there is less concern for the length of the entry. Nevertheless, you should keep Web site index entries as succinct as possible without impinging on the meaning. Users can scan the entries quickly if they are not too wordy. Users are also accustomed to concise entries from back-of-the-book indexes. I suggest a length of one to four words, although there is no hard-and-fast rule for this. In fact, proper nouns, such as organization names, may consist of more words. With a single column, you also have the additional space to add parenthetical notes or qualifiers as part of the entry. The index entries can definitely give more detail than the extremely concise labels found on a Web site's navigation menu tabs or buttons.

The width of a Web page depends on the user's monitor size, screen resolution settings, and browser window sizing. To accommodate the largest number of users, those with standard monitor size and resolution settings, you should assume a maximum width of 500 pixels on a page, which is about 92 characters at a browser's default font style and size. You only need to be concerned with this, though, if the index has multiple columns. Otherwise, the text will automatically wrap at the right end of the screen no matter what the view size is.

If you base your main entries on Web page headings, then you need to capture the main topic in a concise phrase, which may differ substantially from a wordier heading. The headings listed here are some of the subheadings found within the section "Choosing Which Headings to Index" in Chapter 7. You will notice that they are quite long. If you were to construct indexer terms from them, you would need to word them more concisely. I have suggested concise main entries for each boldface heading. Remember, a good index should have multiple variant terms to give users other possible logical entry points.

Whether there is significant amount of information

Suggested index entries: quantity of content

content quantity

information quantity

Whether information is too detailed, trivial, or off-topic for the site

Suggested index entries: relevance of content

content relevance

Whether content within a section has a special focus and audience

Suggested index entry: audience of content

First Word of Phrase

These examples bring us to the next point: word order within an entry. Keeping in mind the alphabetical arrangement of an index, terms that consist of more than one word should have at the beginning a prominent keyword that is likely to be looked up. Terms should not begin with articles, prepositions, question words, or common adjectives such as: few, some, most, many, all, another, and so on. This same philosophy applies to book indexing. An example of a heading whose first word requires changing in an index term is the following:

Determining the keywords

Users are probably not going to look up the word "determining." This phrase, therefore, should be changed for the index term to:

keywords, determining

It is also better to avoid overuse of a starting word for a term that is excessively common within the site, such as "indexing" in the case of this book. This is because there would be so many entries starting with "indexing." That is not to say that it would be wrong to have the term "indexing home pages," but it should be avoided, and the alternate term "home pages, indexing of" is also needed.

Term Clarity and Context

Because terms in an index appear somewhat out of context, clarity is essential. If index terms are based upon headings within a page, keep in mind that headings may be worded in a very simple manner due to the framework of the page. For example, if you look at the subheadings that appear later in this chapter under "Formatting Subentry Indentation," you notice that some of the headings lack context:

Line Spacing
Use of Bullets
Use of Style Sheets

To enhance clarity, the words "indexes" should be added to each, such as:

spacing in indexes
bullets in indexes
style sheets for indexes

These short phrases are still easy for a reader to skim, yet enhance the initial term with distinguishable meaning.

Term Grammar

Main entries should be nouns or verbal nouns (gerunds), those ending in "ing," such as "writing." Common nouns should be plural if countable, such as "policies." Terms may start with an adjective preceding the noun, as long as the words constitute a phrase that is likely to be looked up. An example would be "restricted areas." If a heading begins with a verb, it should be changed. For example the heading:

Prepare a sample index

should be changed to:

sample index preparation

"Preparation" is too weak to act as the keyword, because it is not likely to be looked up for this purpose.

CREATING SUBENTRIES
Single Subentries

The requirement of only one URL locator per entry in Web site indexing not only has the potential for a greater number of subentries, but can also result in a single subentry under a main entry (or a single sub-subentry under a subentry). Although in book indexing, a main entry with a single subentry is considered undesirable, the peculiar requirements of Web site indexes make it acceptable in this medium. When there is both a general discussion of a topic on one Web page and a more specific discussion on a different Web page, this is indexed with the main entry for the general discussion and the main entry plus a single subentry for the more specific discussion. In book indexing, both pages would be cited at the single entry of the main entry, with no subentry.

Despite the greater need for subentries in Web site indexing, due to the need for different index entries for each URL locator, some Web site indexes end up having relatively few subentries compared to book indexes. This occurs because the average size of Web sites is smaller than that of the average book, so fewer subentries are needed. Also, if some content of the Web site is known to be changing, you do not want to make such specific entries. More general entries will remain valid.

Subentry Structure Not to Mimic Web Page Internal Link Structure

Some Web pages have a lot of content requiring subsections with headings. These headings may be repeated near the top of the page with jump links to each of the sections below. In these instances, the headings are probably suitable for indexing, and the sections below them may be indexed with the section name as the basis for the main entry. There is no need, however to also index these sections with the main page topic as the main entry and each section heading topic as a subentry. The index entry and subentries would become redundant with the internal navigation within the page.

For example, the "Reference Sources on the Internet" page on the ASI Web site (www.asindexing.org/site/refbooks.shtml) lists resource links by category. Each category serves as a heading linked to from a list at the top of the page. The following categories are included:

Dictionaries, Thesauri, and Other Language Tools

Encyclopedias, Collections of Information, and Fact Books
Phone Directories, Organizational Listings, and Geographical Maps
Of Particular Interest to Indexers
Additional Lists of General Reference Sites

Each of the above headings has a main entry in the ASI site index with a link to its anchor within the Reference Sources page. None of the headings, however, is listed as a subentry to the main entry **term references sources, list of online**, which links to the top of the Reference Sources page. There is simply no need, because the list of headings appears neatly at the top of that page.

In fact, it is preferable to have the section-heading links within the page, rather than as subentries to a main entry in the index. The latter would require clicking back and forth between the index and the desired page. The user would rather jump between links within the same page than have to go back and forth to a different (index) page.

Non-Indented Subentries

Some site indexes on the Web do not use indented subentries. This happens because, without the benefits of using indexing software, it is easier to create indexes with no indenting. To display terms with a second level of specificity in these circumstances, colons may serve as visual clues, as shown in the example from the Berkeley Lab index (www.lbl.gov/lab-index/a-master.html):

Maps: Directions and Maps on How to Get to the Lab
Maps: Berkeley Lab Site Map
Maps: Offsite Lab Shuttle Bus Map
Maps: Onsite Lab Shuttle Bus Map

Dashes can indicate sublevel relationships, as in Monash University Arts Faculty index (www.arts.monash.edu.au/alpha.html):

German Studies — Languages, Cultures and Linguistics
German Studies — Undergraduate — Areas of Study — Current Students

Subentries may also be set off by commas or as parenthetical information. None of these visually show the structure as clearly as an indented style. It is just easier to browse an index with indents, and I encourage you to use indented subentries.

Sub-Subentries (Third-Level Entries)

Occasionally, the index structure demands a third level of indexing, indented under subentries (called sub-subentries). A larger index for a larger site more likely calls for third-level entries than one for a small site.

The single column design in most Web site indexes makes additional levels of the index easier to read than in the narrow format of a two-column index. In Web indexes with single columns, third and fourth levels can display without wrapping.

When creating subentries and sub-subentries in Web indexes, however, you want to avoid adding so many subentries and sub-subentries that the list gets longer than the screen view and the main entry can no longer be seen on the screen. Fewer lines can be seen on the screen than on a printed page, only about 25–30 lines in default font or 550–650 pixels in height. If you end up with too many lines of subentries, try reducing the font size slightly (don't make it too small) or restructure the index, so that you promote one or more subentries to a main heading status. If you take this tact, add *See* references to guide the index user to these outplaced entries.

In Web site indexes, third-level entries often distinguish between multiple instances of a subentry, which in a book index could simply get different page numbers. Sub-subentries are supported in dedicated book indexing software and in HTML Indexer, but not in XrefHT.

Subentries for Multiple Locators

The greatest difference between printed indexes and Web site indexes is that a single entry in a printed index may have multiple locators, i.e., multiple page numbers, while a hypertext entry can link to only one destination.

As you create your index, you might end up with two identically worded entries linked to different URLs. You will notice this when you alphabetically sort the records prior to generating the index. Any indexing tool permits repeated terms with different locators, and you could even proceed with generating a Web site index with more than one identically worded entry, but the resulting repeated terms would not be helpful to the user. You must differentiate the index entries or even consider removing one.

If you repeat the main entry, simply add a subentry to one or both to distinguish them. If you have repeated subentries, you may add a sub-subentry to one or both, or you may reword the subentries to differentiate them. You need to take care, though, not to let the distinction between similar subentries become too obscure.

You don't have to use further indented sub-subentries if you don't want to. You could try other methods such as parenthetical qualifiers as shown in the BBC index of radio and television programs (Figure 8.1). In this index excerpt, notice how the indexer differentiated multiple references on Art. Even the general page is given a name: "Art homepage."

You may also consider removing a second occurrence of the entry in the instance where only brief, introductory information is presented on a topic that later comes up and is expanded upon. Unlike a book index, which tends to cover a topic more thoroughly with all pertinent references to the text, a Web site index can be more selective and is not held to the same standard of comprehensiveness.

- **Arsenal**

- Arsenal (BBC London)
- Arsenal (BBC Sport)

- **Art**

- Art (Ages 4-11)
- Art (BBC Learning)
- Art (Blast)
- Art (CBBC)
- Art homepage

- **Art (collective)**

- **Art Crime**

Figure 8.1

As it turns out, the issue of how to handle multiple undifferentiated locators in hypertext is a greater problem in theory than in practice. In my experience with ordinary Web sites, I have not found it a serious problem. Perhaps Web sites are written more concisely than books and don't repeat information as often. Indeed, the linear nature of printed documentation requires a concept to be introduced, then discussed in detail, and then summarized (the old "tell them what you're going to tell them, then tell it to them, and finally tell them what you told them" approach). Web content, by contrast, tends to "cut to the chase." If you were indexing a book converted to HTML, however, you face a greater problem of multiple locators.

You need to take a different approach when indexing Web sites compared to books. In book indexing, you begin by assuming that you will have multiple page numbers for most entries, and you only start considering subentries when you realize that the list of locators will exceed five or six. For book indexers, trying to anticipate whether there will be sufficient instances of a topic to justify creating subentries for it makes the job a challenge. In Web site indexing, you know that each indexable topic/locator/URL must have its own unique index entry, so right from the start you write each entry as specifically as possible. When you sort records in the end, you may then decide that some entries don't need such specificity and edit them accordingly.

Entries in Periodical Web Indexes

How to handle multiple entries for the same topic in Web site indexes becomes much more of an issue when dealing with any kind of periodical, whether an online version of a print magazine, a zine, or merely a collection of some newsletter-type articles within a larger Web site. As long as the site contains dated Web pages, new ones added to the collection rather than replacing older pages, topics will inevitably recur.

Among the methods to handle multiple entries on the same topic are:

- Repeated entries differentiated by date
- Multiple dates following the entry
- Entry links to an intermediate page

Repeated Entries Differentiated by Date

Identically named entries to different sources, when coming from periodical sources, can be distinguished by the addition of a publication date, typically expressed in brief numerical format.

In the index example in Figure 8.2, extracted from the *Consumer Reports* index, identical subentries for "number portability" are differentiated by date.

```
Telephone service
    bills, deciphering (FREE) 2/05
    cellular (Ratings) 1/06
        call forwarding 2/04
        complaints (FREE) 7/05
        coverage (FREE) 2/02
        911 service (FREE) 1/06
        music 5/06
        number portability (FREE) 2/04
        number portability (FREE) 12/03
        service problems (FREE) 1/06
```

Figure 8.2

If you add a date to differentiate repeated entries, you do not need to modify the text too, as is demonstrated by the awkward phrasing in the example in Figure 8.3, extracted from the Los Alamos National Laboratory Web site index. Notice the first two subentries under Oxford English Dictionary: "again available online" and "available online." At a minimum, this would seem to call for a switch in the order of the subentries to run them chronologically, although periodical indexes often favor providing the most recent issue first. Furthermore, a look at the source text suggests that the more recent citation has no new information and therefore does not even need an entry.

```
overdue notices via email (12/97)
Oxford English Dictionary
    again available online (11/01)
    available online (3/01)
    new terms added (2/04)
    online trial (5/00)
```

Figure 8.3

Multiple Dates Following the Entry

Another way to indicate multiple identically worded entries with different dates uses a single entry with multiple dates following. The dates instead of the entry then serve as the hyperlinks. This is the case in the example in Figure 8.4, extracted from the index of the journal *Rochester History*. Here, the different dates and volume/issue numbers (or links) are separated from each other by a semicolon.

```
Abbott, Mrs. Helen Probst
    city manager movement and-1920s, 23(3):22 (Jul 1961); 32(2):3 (Apr 1970)
    club membership, 10(2&3):22 (Jul 1948); 31(1):23 (Jan 1969)
    as suffragist, 10(2&3):20, 21, 22 (Jul 1948)
ABC. See Action for a Better Community
Abendpost (newspaper)
    immigrants and, 64(3):8 (Sum 2002)
```

Figure 8.4

Entry Links to an Intermediate Page

Although not very common on Web sites, but found in online subscription periodical databases (such as InfoTrac or EBSCOHost), the entry with multiple locators can link to an intermediate page or frame that provides a citation list of the actual pages. You cannot implement this with simple hypertext links, though. You need to have a database, and the hypertext calls up a database query.

In the example in Figure 8.5 from the Montague Institute Review, the index entry licensing is selected in the index frame on the left, then the list of Web documents for this topic are displayed in the frame on the right.

EDITING THE INDEX

Always allow time to edit your index, no matter the type of index. Edit as much as possible while still using the indexing program, where you have sorting and other manipulation features available. You may directly edit the final HTML index output using HTML editing software, or just by editing the code manually, but you

126 Indexing Specialties: Web Sites

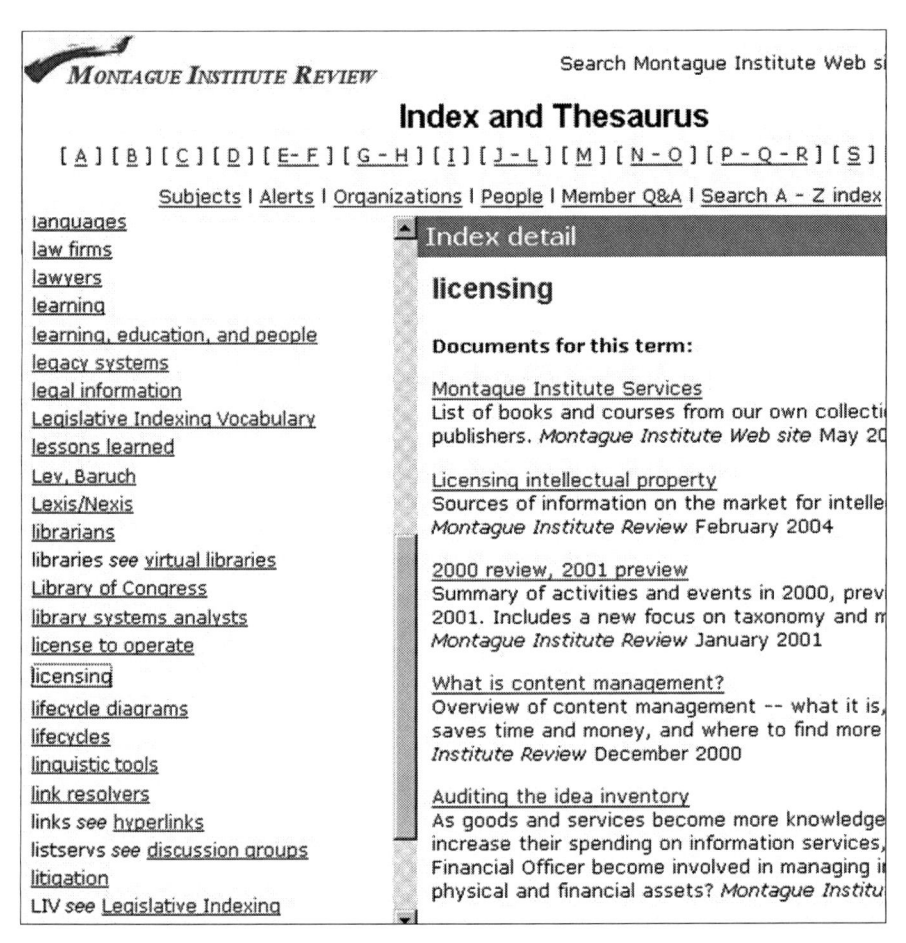

Figure 8.5

cannot edit an HTML file with the indexing software. As mentioned previously, HTML Indexer imbeds the index terms in the page files. If you change the terms in the generated HTML index instead, the software cannot update the pages. The index will still work, but you lose the advantage of HTML Indexer's feature that keeps track of changes and automatically deletes from the index any entries to files that get removed. (See earlier discussion in the final section of Chapter 6.)

I recommend, while indexing, to periodically view what the generated index would look like while you still have your indexing program open and running so that you can easily make changes there:

- If using HTML Indexer, anytime during the indexing process you can view what the output index looks like by selecting from the menu **View > Output file**.

- If using XRefHT, anytime during the indexing process you can view what the output index looks like by selecting from the menu **Tools > Preview in browser**.

In either case, make a note of what you want to change and then go back to the list of terms to make the desired changes.

Following is a basic checklist of some of the things to watch for when editing an index, beyond spell checking and basic typo editing:

- All terms are either distinct with distinct links or they are deliberate double postings with the same links. There are no slight variations of the same term, such as singular/plural, participle/noun forms of the same term, and so on.
- All subentries also have been made into main entries as double postings, where the terms constitute strong concepts to stand on their own and are likely entry points for users.
- Unlinked main entries have more than a single subentry. Convert single subentries under unlinked main entries into the main heading.
- Terms start with keywords that are likely to be looked up.
- Variant terms (double postings) are not redundant within a few lines of each other.
- The list of subentries (along with any sub-subentries) does not exceed one screen view (25 lines).
- The cross-references are validated: There are no circular references, no blind references, no misuse of *See* vs. *See also*, and there is sufficient information to merit cross-references as opposed to double posting.

INDEX FORMAT OPTIONS

Since Web indexes are relatively new, there are no editorial standards for the format style. Decisions regarding format and editorial style remain up to the Web site or intranet owner. Since the site has probably never included an index before, the site owner may not have specific opinions regarding format and style. Thus, the indexer has greater freedom of decision for Web site indexes than for print products. It is also much easier for the Web site indexer to implement the formatting options on a Web site than in a printed publication, whether through the indexing tool or with HTML editing software afterward. In the following sections, I'll refer to the site owner as the client, even if it is an internal client in the case where the indexer is an employee.

Although there are no standard formats or styles for Web indexes, just as there are no editorial standards of any kind for the Web, conventions do exist, which over time will probably become more established. Editorial formatting includes the placement of heading letters, use of columns, placement of top-of-page links, and case of entries.

Heading Letters

The list of the letters of the alphabet to jump to each letter section is typically located at the top of the index or top of each index page. A second placement at the bottom of the page is rare, since a "back to top" link can bring the user back to the list. Some indexes have the list of letters at the beginning of each letter section, but this can appear to be too frequent, if several letters contain very few entries.

Putting the letters in a separate frame, while not as common, is a nice feature, as in the American Society of Indexers site index. This "freezes" the ribbon of letters at the top of the user's browser window even when scrolling down through the index. It is even possible to put the letters on every page of a Web site, either in a frame or just in the Web page heading/menu area. While it saves the user one click, having the heading letters on every page of the site becomes distracting and a poor use of screen real estate.

As for grouping letters or omitting letters that have no entries under them, such as Q or X, that is entirely up to you or your client.

If the index is long, with so many entries per letter of the alphabet that each letter section typically takes up at least two scrolling screens, it might be a good idea to create ranges within each letter (such as **Aa–Af, Af–Ap, Ar–Az**). Web indexing tools, however, do not offer this as an option, so you would have to create this feature manually afterward. This finer level of segmentation can make maintaining the index more complicated. The British Go Association Index uses regular heading letters, but within each letter page provides more specific ranges for each letter. For example, if you click on the **K** page, at the top of the page you may select from:

Ki | Kn | Ko

If the index is long, it may also be desirable to break it up with a Web page for each letter of the alphabet. Although it does not make that much difference, Web site designers and users tend to dislike excessively long pages. If you have graphic images within the site index (such as "return to top" arrows), a very long index page could take more time to load.

Columns

Book indexes typically employ two columns to save space. While HTML Indexer offers multiple columns as an option, I recommend avoiding it. There is no need to save space online. It's much easier for the user to scroll down through the index page just once, than to have to jump up to the top to scroll down a second time. Users might not like being unable to see the bottom of one column and the top of the next column at the same time.

Multiple columns may be used on Web pages if the entire index page fits into little more than one screen view. If this is done, though, there is little need for letters with jump links to the letter section. Another format is to keep one letter heading per column, as in the U.S. Food and Drug Administration index (www.fda.gov/opacom/hpchoice.html). Another exception to the rule of avoiding two-column indexes might be when each column is in a separate language to serve different users, as is the case of the Indexing Society of Canada (ISC) site index (www.indexers.ca/siteindex.html), whose index is in French and English.

Note, though, that when you generate your index to review it, it won't necessarily look the same as when it becomes part of the Web site. It is likely that there will be a graphical header and a navigation menu, perhaps on the left side. This would push the index down and possibly over to the right, so there might be not much extra space for additional columns after all.

"Return to Top of Page" Links

Although not entirely necessary since there is a scrollbar, "return to top of page" links are convenient for the user. In creating these links, you need to consider:

- **Wording** – "return to top," "back to top," "top of page," etc.
- **Position** – Only at the bottom, after every letter, or after every few letters; flush left or flush right
- **Appearance** – The use of graphic arrows; or with styles you can make hypertext "return to top of page" links a different color from hypertext index entries

Making the "return to top" links distinct in appearance from the index entries is a good idea. You can make them flush right instead of left, use a different font style and/or color, or use graphic arrows instead of text. HTML Indexer has a feature to automatically insert a graphic file for "back-to-top" links.

Case of Entries

As in book indexing style, you may prefer to use lowercase for index entries that are not proper nouns. As some proper nouns will inevitably be included within the index, the use of lowercase for the rest makes the proper nouns, such as names of organizations, stand out to users. On the other hand, you might want to distinguish all main headings by using initial capital letters. In print this practice is more helpful since print typically uses narrow columns and has line wraps. Online, where one column is the typical layout, that issue becomes less of a problem. The decision can be made on an index-by-index basis depending on the depth and complexity of the index.

Furthermore, since some so-called site indexes contain merely an alphabetical sorting of Web page titles, which tend to be uppercase, use of lowercase makes it clear to the user that these are original topics and not merely page titles.

Special Pages

Users expect every hyperlinked index entry to take them to the referred Web page in the site. It aggravates users if the entry links to a page that they are restricted from accessing or requires the launching of their PDF (portable document format) reader software when they didn't expect it. Some Web sites have portions restricted to members with password access. While there could be separate indexes of public and private sections, it's easier to create just one index. Links to restricted pages can be indicated in the index with a notation or a graphic symbol, such as a padlock or a key. Similarly, the use of small icons, such as of an Adobe Acrobat page, to indicate PDF files is a nice touch in indexes that have hypertext entries linking directly to PDF documents.

Modifying the Generated Index

You can always modify the format and style of the index after it is generated by making changes in your HTML editor. The heading letter size, font style, color, justification, use of a horizontal rule, etc., are all style decisions that you can leave up to your client.

Modifications to the actual index entries are also possible, but this results in more work when it comes to maintaining and updating the index. For example, different font sizes, styles, or faces might be used to further distinguish main headings from subentries. In the University of Missouri-Columbia Information Access and Technology Services index excerpt in Figure 8.6, main headings are in bold, whereas subentries are in plain text.

FORMATTING SUBENTRY INDENTATION

As Chapter 3 showed, there are several methods for achieving indented subentries:
- Repeated "nonbreaking" spaces
- Definition lists
- Unordered lists (typically bulleted)
- Styles and classes (with divisions)

Which Indexing Software Supports Which Indenting Formats

While the format and method for indenting index entries should not be the determining factor in choosing an indexing tool, it may still play a role. Following is a list summarizing the indexing tools discussed or mentioned in earlier chapters and what kind of formatting method each employs for indenting the subentries.

R

Radio Services, Two-Way
- Equipment

Registry, Computer

Reporting Security Problems

Research Network

Research Support Computing
- Internet2
- MU Research Network

Resource Accounts

Responders Training
- Course Schedule
- Membership
- Certification Testing

Figure 8.6

- No indexing tool; just a word processor and an HTML editor
  - All formatting options possible
- HTML-generated output from CINDEX or SKY Index
  - Repeated nonbreaking spaces (no bullets)
- HTML-generated output from Macrex
  - All formatting options possible
- HTML/Prep used with any indexing program
  - Unordered lists without bullets (default)
  - Unordered lists with bullets
  - Definition lists (no bullets) for main entries and unordered lists with bullets for subentries
  - HTML heading tags (<h1> to <h6>), whose attributes you may specify in a style sheet
- FAR HTML Help
  - Classes and style sheets
- XrefHT

- Unordered lists with bullets
- HTML Indexer
  - Repeated nonbreaking spaces (no bullets)
  - Classes and style sheets

For the client, the method itself may not matter as much as the output appearance. Will the index be double-spaced or single-spaced? Will it have bullets or not? The client may also have an opinion or policy on the use of style sheets.

Line Spacing

It is preferable for indexes to be single-spaced. It benefits the user to see as much of the index as possible in one screen view. If there are many subentries and sub-subentries, the user will less likely feel lost in the index if more of the index can be seen to give context. The user might also notice other topics of potential interest. Furthermore, more entries per screen require less scrolling. Even though there will be links to jump to the start of a chosen letter of the alphabet, the desired entry could still fall far down the list within the letter section. Finally, the index is more recognizable as an index when more of it can be displayed at once. While some Web site indexes use paragraphs for each main entry and lists for subentries (resulting in double spacing between main entries and single-spaced subentries), the majority of Web site indexes have single spacing for the entire index.

The client may request double-spaced main entries with lists of single-spaced subentries. This would be due to greater familiarity with and expectations in Web content design than in index design. In Web text content, it is typical to have headings for lists set off from other headings by a blank line (paragraph break). It is also possible that an earlier index was created with double-spaced main entries and single-spaced subentries, because the indexer did not use an indexing tool. The client should be made aware of the fact that the index is a very different page from the rest of the site and need not follow the style conventions for typical content pages. (This is also the case for back-of-the-book indexes.) Of course, you can also tell the client that indexing tools, which facilitate the indexing process, create indexes without the extra space between main entry lines.

In the example in Figure 8.7, the index has double spacing between main entries and single spacing between subentries. In this particular case this format was deemed acceptable, because many headings have multiple subentries. Double spacing main entries would not be as desirable if subentries were few, which is more typical for Web site indexes.

Use of Bullets

There is no preferred style for Web indexes with respect to bullets. Whether they facilitate the browsing of the index is open to debate. Although printed indexes

```
• sh
    ○ changing environment variables for
    ○ changing prompt for
    ○ changing shell variables for

• shell
    ○ changing
    ○ definition of
    ○ different types of
    ○ features provided by
    ○ metacharacters
    ○ programming with See shell script

• SHELL variable
```

Figure 8.7

don't have bullets, users are accustomed to seeing bullets on the Web and its graphic quality makes information easy to follow. In terms of Web indexes, bulleted lists are popular because they offer an easy way to create indenting when not using a Web indexing tool.

The client may request bulleted entries, but again this is likely due to the client's familiarity with and expectations in Web content design, rather than index design. If you use a tool that can create bulleted indexes, that is fine. If you use a tool that does not generate a bulleted index, though, tell your client that the perceived and minimal benefits of bullets are more than offset by the time saved by using an indexing tool.

Use of Style Sheets

Styles sheets apply to more than just indenting of subentries; they are used for all kinds of formatting on a Web page. The use of classes and styles for your index, which HTML Indexer supports, allows more control over the index, especially for future revisions of the index format. For this reason, the client may prefer use of a style sheet. There are other advantages to style sheets in general, so even if your client doesn't raise this issue, you should ask. If, however, neither you nor your client is comfortable with style sheets, you don't have to bother with them. It's also possible that some style classes will not be supported in older browsers, but this is decreasingly the case.

Classes and styles have the benefit of controlling the appearance of other components of the index page. For example, with styles you can change the appearance of hyperlinks, so that not all of the hyperlinks within a page appear the same (by default blue and underlined). You might want to make index entries in one color, cross-references in a second color, and "top of page" links in a third color.

CONCLUSION

In deciding the appearance of a Web site index, there are some formatting options that you can control in your Web indexing software, and there are other formatting changes that you can make only in your HTML editing software. You may also decide to use a style sheet to control these aspects of the index Web page. There are more formatting options in a Web page index than a printed index, including the use of color and graphics. With so many formatting decisions to make, it's a good idea to examine other Web site indexes to see what looks appealing and what does not. A linked list of Web site indexes is available on the Web site of the Web Indexing Special Interest Group of the American Society of Indexers (www.web-indexing.org/web-index-examples.htm).

FURTHER READING

The following books are on indexing techniques in general and are not specific to web site indexing, but are still helpful for their guidelines in how to fashion index entries.

Booth, Pat F. *Indexing: The Manual of Good Practice*. London: K. G. Saur, 2001.

Borko, Harold and Charles L. Bernier. *Indexing Concepts and Methods*. New York: Academic Press, 1978.

Chicago Manual of Style, 15th edition. Chicago: University of Chicago Press, 2003.

Cleveland, Donald B. *Introduction to Indexing and Abstracting*. Englewood, CO: Libraries Unlimited, 1990.

Fetters, Linda K. *Handbook of Indexing Techniques: A Guide for Beginning Indexers*, 3rd ed. Corpus Christi, TX: FIM-Books, 2001.

Knight, G. Norman. *Indexing, The Art of*. Boston: Allen & Unwin, 1979.

Lancaster, F. W. *Indexing and Abstracting in Theory and Practice*. 3rd edition. Champaign, IL: University of Illinois Graduate School of Library and Information Science/Facet Publishing, 2003.

Mulvany, Nancy C. *Indexing Books*, 2nd edition. Chicago: University of Chicago Press, 2005.

Smith, Sherry and Kari Kells. *Inside Indexing: The Decision-Making Process*. Bend, OR: Northwest Indexing Press, 2005.

Stauber, Do Mi. *Facing the Text: Content and Structure in Book Indexing*. Eugene, OR: Cedar Row Press, 2004.

Thatcher, Virginia. *Indexes: Writing, Editing, Production*. Lanham, MD: Scarecrow Press, 1995.

Wellisch, Hans. *Indexing from A to Z*, 2nd edition. New York: H. W. Wilson, 1995.

Chapter 9

Web Index Market and Business

If you are already a freelance indexer, then you are probably interested in adding Web site indexing work to your freelance repertoire. Although the freelance market for Web site indexes is not well developed, that will probably change in the future. As a start, it's a good idea to know what kinds of sites are best suited for indexes and what the competition is from other search techniques. In addition to an overview of the market, this chapter also provides marketing tips, rate information, index maintenance considerations, and discussion list resources.

TYPES OF WEB SITES SUITABLE FOR INDEXING

In book indexing, almost all nonfiction books can and probably should have indexes. This is not the case with Web sites. Some are too small or too large, some change too frequently, and some have content better searched through a taxonomy or a database rather than a traditional alphabetical index. Whether you are a freelancer trying to decide how to market your services or you are employed by an organization that maintains a Web site, you need to consider various factors before deciding whether a Web site needs an index.

Size Considerations

Extremely small Web sites do not require indexes, and indeed a very small index does not work well. A Web site of less than 15 or 20 pages should probably not be indexed. I would suggest a minimum size of 25 pages. But this also depends on how much information the pages contain. In any Web site, there will be some pages not suitable for indexing. When looking for Web sites on which to practice indexing, you can look for those of 25–50 pages.

Extremely large sites also pose a problem. For Web sites or intranets of over a 1,000 pages, not only is it a lot of work, but by the time an index is complete, the site will likely have changed. A very long index might also be less practical to browse through, even with a separate index page for each letter of the alphabet. This does not mean that large sites should not include indexes. Rather than indexing the entire site, individual indexes can be applied to individual subsections.

Although Web pages can vary greatly in length and the amount of indexable content they contain, you can still consider Web site page count as roughly comparable to book page count. Therefore, Web sites of several hundred pages are quite practical to index, just as are books of the same size.

Changeability

A major issue that you face in Web site indexing is that, unlike printed materials, Web sites and intranets can change frequently. Content within pages changes. New pages are added and old ones are deleted from time to time. Web sites that change especially frequently, such as a Web site dedicated to a special event, should be avoided in indexing. A Web site that has evolving sections could still be indexed. You should omit pages known to be temporary and refer to pages whose content changes by general topic of the pages only and not specifics.

Rich and Varied Content

A site rich in content and with a variety of content is better suited for indexing. Some sites may have a sufficient number of pages, but insufficient indexable content. These would include pages that display mostly images (for graphic effect rather than as content), components of online games, or short directory entries.

Sites that contain a lot of content, but all of a similar type, such as a catalog of products or a directory of names or organizations, are also not so suitable for indexes. In some cases, all the information can easily be arranged in a categorization scheme. A directory-type site might require an alphabetical list of names to look up, but this is not what we are considering as subject indexing.

Most sites that sell products do not need indexes if most of the pages comprise a listing of products. Potential customers tend to look up products by category, not by alphabetical names. The sites of retailers that offer a confusing mix of products and services, however, would be very appropriate for indexes. For example, a retailer that not only sells products, but also provides delivery and installation, offers service and maintenance contracts, has its own charge card, and/or provides a gift registry, could benefit from an index on its site.

For information-oriented Web sites, an index works better with a broad scope than with a narrow scope. For example, a travel site about a specific region that covers topics of points of interest, accommodations, food, weather, cultural customs, local history, and transportation services would have a broader scope and be more appropriate for an index than a site that just lists points of interests. A site with such a narrow scope could easily be searched by its menu hierarchy, making an index superfluous.

Web sites of online periodicals ought to have some kind of index. But if the periodical has a very narrow focus and a limited number of issues, it is possible that a simple categorization scheme would better serve users.

Repeat Visitors

Web sites that tend to get repeat visitors make especially good candidates for indexes. They are analogous to reference-type books that researchers repeatedly go back to and where an index is especially appreciated. Of course, an index can be useful on Web sites that receive many one-time visitors, but often the objective of such Web sites is to draw in the visitor to explore the site, rather than come in, get information, and then leave. If the Web site owner wants visitors to explore and visit many pages, then the owner is not likely to be very interested in having an index created for the site. Sites that have high repeat visitors, and thus are good candidates for indexes, include company intranets visited by employees, educational institutions by students, organizations by members, and municipal sites by residents.

WEB INDEX MARKET OVERVIEW

Chapter 1 described three types of Web site indexes:

- Indexes of book-like documents that are on Web sites or intranets or e-books
- Indexes of entire general Web sites or subsites
- Periodical indexes that are online or newsletter sections of Web sites

Let's look at the market for each of these in turn and also more closely examine intranets.

Book-Like Documents

Book-like documents on the Web are rare and tend to come from volunteer creations. If an entire book is offered for free access on the Web, then there probably isn't any money to hire an indexer. If you are looking for a volunteer job for the experience, though, consider this type of site. Perhaps at some point in the future, when the Web offers more subscription or pay-per-view content, the business can afford to pay for indexing. Book-like documents on intranets, on the other hand, provide a good market for indexing. These would include various policy manuals and handbooks. There is more information on intranets later.

In addition to book-like documents on the Web, e-books are a relatively new and growing phenomenon. These are electronic books for downloading and reading on a computer or another electronic device. They might seem like a good market, but various factors make the indexing of e-books unlikely for now. First of all, most e-books are fiction. For those that are nonfiction, standards of quality, such as including true indexes rather than just search features for the books, are still not developed. There might be a market in reference-type e-books, though. More significantly, most e-books do not even come in HTML format. HTML is just one of several formats for e-books, including PDF, Microsoft Word, Microsoft Reader, Palm Reader, Rocket Edition, Hiebook, Mobipocket Reader, and Softbook Editions. Furthermore, most e-books are not created from scratch; they are converted from existing print books, which may already have an index. The printed index with its page locators, however, serves no purpose in the e-book version. Unless the index was created by means of embedded indexing and the tagged indexing can be converted to the e-book format, the index for the printed version tends not to be saved in the e-book. Creating a new index for an existing book often might not seem worth the time and effort for the e-book publisher.

Web Sites

Web sites can be classified as commercial and noncommercial. Commercial sites tend either to sell products or services or to provide general corporate information. Although there is a lot of money in retail sites, these are not as likely to need indexes, since the products can fall into categorical arrangements instead. General corporate sites, on the other hand, represent a better market for Web site indexes, although they have some obstacles of their own. Some corporate Web sites are too large and fast-changing to be indexed in detail. Corporate site owners might also prefer a top-level navigation menu with each tab to guide each kind of user and not want a single index to serve all the varied visitors (clients, vendors, competitors, investors, job-seekers, etc.). These subsections could certainly offer their own indexes, though. Perhaps the best market for Web site indexes among commercial sites comes from sites that regularly serve repeat visitors who want to look up specific information quickly. These tend to be sites of service companies, whose customers are long-term members or subscribers, such as banks, insurance companies, medical plans, telecommunications services, or utilities.

Noncommercial sites include government, educational institutions, and nonprofit organization sites. State and federal agency Web sites contain a great deal of information, and users tend to want to look up something quickly rather than to spend time browsing around. A number of these sites have indexes already, but these need improving and updating, and new Web site sections get added. Getting government contracts can be complicated, though. Internet work might be contracted to a company, which in turn might hire an indexer as a subcontractor. In either case, you might need to get listed in a government contractor's directory first.

Another significant market for Web site indexing is the Web sites of colleges and universities. In fact, a search on Google for "A–Z index" or "A–Z site index" reveals that higher education institutions own the sites with perhaps the overall largest number of indexes. In addition to the institutions themselves, other educational resources on the Web also make likely candidates for indexes, due to their high level of standards to inform and educate.

Nonprofit organization sites are well suited for indexes, since they tend to encompass lots of varied content. The problem is that they usually cannot afford to hire freelance Web site indexers. The larger, well-endowed national-level nonprofit organizations thus constitute a better market for Web site indexing.

Periodicals

Online periodicals represent a good market for Web indexes. Commercial periodical publishers increasingly offer access to their back issues of publications for their subscribers. They may even make the access free, but then it is more limited. Organizations that issue newsletters are also likely to include them on the Web site.

Typically, past issues of a periodical can be found on the Web site under the menu item "Archives." If the periodical has an index, this is where it would be found. Often, when there is no index, you will find the articles are merely listed by issue date and probably grouped by year. Usually, periodical issues online only go back to the late 1990s, when Web publishing came to the fore.

If the collection of back issues is large, the same subject frequently recurs. Then, a database approach tends to work better than a back-of-the-book style browsable index. A database index can also be dynamic and updated with the indexing of each new issue. If the collection of back issues is not so great and the periodical comes out no more frequently than monthly, then a back-of-the-book style index should suffice.

Often when an organization publishes a newsletter both in print and on its Web site, to save the time of converting the content, the newsletter goes up on the Web site only in PDF form. If individual articles are in PDF form, they can still be indexed at the article level. But if an entire issue is one PDF file, you cannot index the individual articles, because you cannot create anchors in the file. Although there are ways to tag or mark a PDF document, these tags cannot be accessed in HTML over the Web.

Index maintenance is an important issue with respect to periodical indexes, and may complicate the idea of contracting a freelance indexer. If the periodical is small, such as an occasional newsletter, it might not seem worth the trouble to retain a freelancer to update the index. A commercial periodical, however, that has a regular number of articles in each issue can be indexed by freelancers, and print periodicals often are indexed this way.

Intranets

While intranets show a great potential for indexes, complications face the indexer. Intranets have rich and varied content and serve repeat users, but intranet content and structure change frequently, perhaps more frequently than the external Web site of the same organization. Intranets also tend to be huge, more like a small version of the World Wide Web with its own numerous Web sites. Many have thousands, tens of thousands, or even more than 100,000 pages. Rather than one index for an entire intranet, multiple indexes are needed for subsites or sections. An alphabetical directory of subsites could also be added. Finally, depending on the organization, intranet work may be kept in-house, rather than contracted out to freelancers.

To manage large intranets, often a content management system (CMS) is used. This kind of software helps organize the HTML documents and offers methods for retrieval, by the assignment of keywords or other metadata. The organization may hire indexers to assign keywords or create a controlled vocabulary of terms, in a task that is more like database indexing than back-of-the-book indexing.

Intranets may be managed within the information technology/information systems (IT/IS) department, although other departments, such as internal/corporate communications, may deal with them. Human resources (HR) departments tend to create the greatest volume of content on an intranet, so if indexes are to be created for subsections, HR might also be the department to contact. Some corporations are starting to create "information management" (IM) or "knowledge management" (KM) departments, which oversee the intranet, among other records and document management.

COMPETITION FROM OTHER SEARCH METHODS

There is a belief among many Web developers and designers that locating information on the relatively new medium of the Web is better served by relatively new methods of search and navigation. While these methods have their purposes, they do not necessarily preclude Web site indexes. To compete and better "sell" the idea of site indexes, it is important to know how these other search and navigation methods differ from site indexes and how indexes remedy their deficiencies.

Search Engines

A major competition to Web site indexes comes from ubiquitous inexpensive or free search. Search engines are becoming more sophisticated, but higher-end search engines cost a lot more. As finding information within a Web site becomes more important and the shortcomings of onsite search engines become more apparent, Web site owners will look for ways to raise the standards of finding information on their sites, and the use of site indexes will be considered.

Site search engines may not retrieve enough or any pages for a given search. Search engines for the entire Web usually produce satisfactory results in the quantity of pages, as users generally want "some information about" a subject, and this need can typically be met by some of the numerous pages retrieved. If the search engine misses many good pages, the user usually does not know or care. Within a Web site, however, the number of pages is relatively small, so a simple search engine search might not yield sufficient or any results, even if there are good pages on the subject. This most likely occurs because the search subject that the user enters is worded differently from the references to that topic within page text.

Search engines often cannot meet the higher standards that searchers have for searches within a site. Searchers of a site may want all the information a site has on a given topic, whereas searches of the entire Web only want—and expect—some information on a topic. Searchers of a site may also want the information to surface more quickly, since they might be looking at a number of sites.

Site search engines typically retrieve too many irrelevant pages. Web search engines usually produce satisfactory results in the quality of articles, since the major search engine companies have developed complicated criteria and algorithms for the retrieval and ranking of pages. The search engines used within a site may not be so sophisticated. They often retrieve pages that include a mere passing mention of the search term but do not really focus on the subject at all. In the end, the quality of the search engine results reflects the sophistication of the search string entered by the user, which cannot be controlled. In the A–Z index, on the other hand, the quality of the results reflects the sophistication of the indexer.

Search engines are indispensable on very large and changing sites. Yet a site benefits from more than one finding tool. This makes sense especially when certain pages of the Web site are deliberately omitted from the index because of their ephemeral nature.

Navigation Menus

The organizational and structural design of a Web site, including its navigation menus, has become an art and science of its own, known as information architecture. Information architects plan out the content of a Web site to ensure it has logical organization so that information is relatively easy to find. The pages of the site are structured and linked into a kind of hierarchy. The navigation menu shows the top of the hierarchy and the next level or two, if there are dropdown submenus. Some information architects mistakenly believe that a site index becomes unnecessary if the navigation structure is well designed. Yet the purpose of a navigation menu differs from searching, since its focus is on navigating, meaning finding one's way around. Searching, on the other hand, means going after precise information. Thus, the navigation menu really should not be considered a rival search method to an index. Information experts recognize the value of multiple ways for users to find the information they want.

Site Maps

Site maps might also be mistakenly confused as serving the same purpose as site indexes. Site maps, in fact, really offer no competition to site indexes, since they act as the table of contents and serve a somewhat different function. Some Web site owners and designers are unaware of the difference, however, and might even mislabel a site map as a "site index." Thus, they may claim their site has an index and doesn't need one, when, in fact, it does not have an index at all.

A site map tends to reflect the hierarchical structure of the Web pages of a site with categorized Web page titles. A goal of a site map is to have a list of a site's Web pages that can be quickly scanned in one screen view (with minimal scrolling), without having to go through each menu and submenu one by one. A site map might not include all the pages of a Web site. If the site is large, only the top few levels of the hierarchy will be displayed. The entries in the site map tend to be the page titles, although they could be modified slightly. Each page in the site is listed in only one place in the site map. Like the navigation menu, the site map aids in navigation rather than searching, and thus should not be seen as an alternative to an index.

The screenshot in Figure 9.1 shows the top excerpted portion of a site map on a public library Web site (www.gleasonlibrary.org). The organization of the site map strictly follows the navigation menu of the Web site. For comparison, the same Web site also has a site index.

You can use software tools to aid in the creation of site maps, by extracting Web page titles along with their hierarchical links within a site. The problem is that some of these tools also offer the feature of alphabetically sorting Web page titles to create

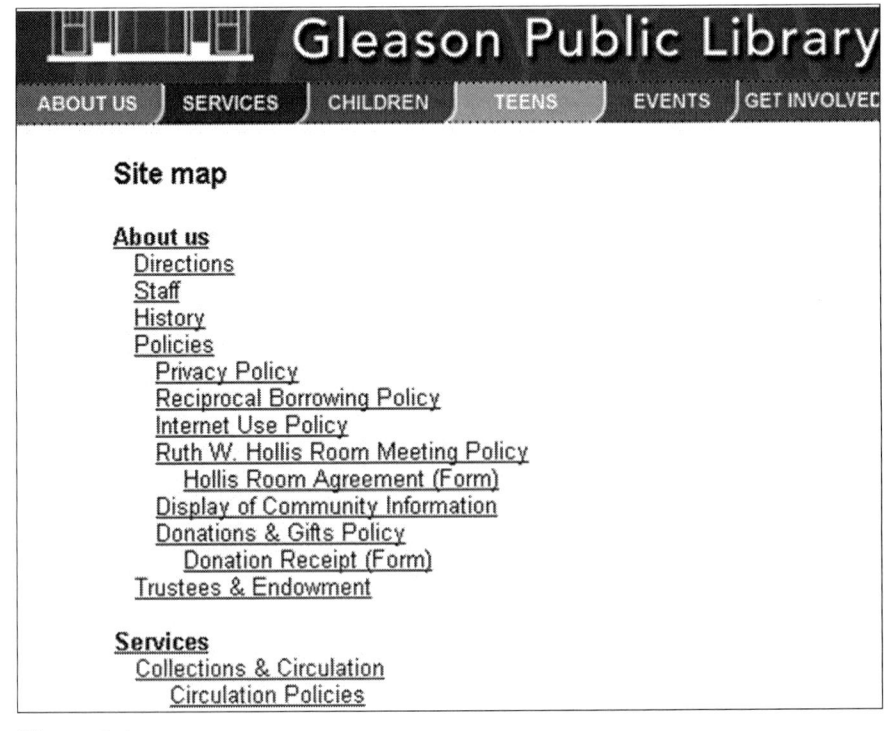

Figure 9.1

a pseudo-index, a feature better not used. An alphabetized list of topics or names is useful, but a list of alphabetized page titles is not. Think of it as an alphabetized table of contents of a book—how useful would that be?

Taxonomies

Taxonomies are hierarchical classifications of terms, concepts, or topics, in a treelike structure, where narrower terms branch out under broader terms. In a Web site taxonomy, the user typically clicks from one level to the next most specific. An example of a very broad taxonomy is that of the Yahoo! directory, or the "yellow pages" category search of a telephone directory Web site. A taxonomy's function and purpose falls somewhere between that of a navigation menu and that of an index. As with an index, the terms or labels of a taxonomy tend to be carefully selected. A narrower concept can be placed in more than one place in the taxonomy. The purpose of a taxonomy is more that of guided search, than for site navigation.

It is extremely rare to find both a taxonomy and an index covering the same content on a Web site. Indexes and taxonomies offer the user different search methods, so ideally both should be implemented on the same content to serve varying user needs. Indeed some periodical article databases subscribed to by libraries offer users both options, such as ProQuest's eLibrary database which offers both a "Search" on indexed keywords and the ability to browse by "Topic." The owners of most Web sites, however, usually don't have the resources to fund the human creation of both a taxonomy and an index on a site.

Certain types of sites or parts of sites are better served by taxonomies while others are better covered by indexes. If most of the content deals with a narrow subject area, such as a Web site devoted to information on a consumer product line, heart disease, or old movies, a taxonomy might work better than an index. An index, on the other hand, serves best a site with varied types of content. Because taxonomies have become the darling of late for aiding the organization and retrieval of information in large Web sites and intranets, they might end up being implemented where an index would actually serve better. For more on taxonomies, see the resources listed at the end of this chapter.

Faceted Search

A faceted search, or faceted browse, involves the selection from a combination of two or more lists of terms on different aspects, or facets, of the content. It's quite effective and easy to use. Several research-oriented sites and retail sites have implemented faceted search. An example is www.shopping.com. For example, after selecting a category of clothing, you then get several facets to simultaneously search, including price range, apparel type, size, online store, material, and brand. The user can combine terms, just as the indexer combines and inverts main entries and subentries. But the faceted search has the advantage over an index of combining more than two concepts at once. A faceted search works well on a collection of documents or records that are of a uniform type and all with the same types of facets. It deals well with a directory of people, companies, or products. While a faceted search is more effective than a simple A–Z index for searching certain kinds of content, the types of Web sites suitable for faceted searching are rather limited. So, while there is a lot of enthusiasm about the effectiveness of faceted search, this search method cannot replace A–Z indexes on most general Web sites.

Educating the Market

What is needed is not merely for Web site indexers to increase their direct marketing efforts, but also for indexers to educate Web site owners, Webmasters, Web site designers, and information architects about the benefits of human-created back-of-the-book style indexes for Web sites. Indexers can do this by publishing articles on Web site indexing (online or in print), giving presentations at meetings of Web professionals, and expressing ideas through various online discussion lists and groups. The Web Indexing SIG of ASI plays a leading role in this endeavor, but individual Web site indexers also need to promote the idea of Web site indexes.

MARKETING FOR THE FREELANCE INDEXER

Marketing services to Web site owners is not as simple as marketing within the established industry of book publishers who know how and why to contract freelance indexers. These suggestions will help you get started:

1. Prepare a sample index.
2. Create or update your own Web site.
3. Offer broader Web-related services.
4. Let your current clients know of your new service.
5. Contact organizations and companies of which you are a member or client.
6. Network locally.
7. Network through the larger Web community.
8. Contact Web design firms.

1. Prepare a Sample Index

For the freelance indexer starting off, creating a sample Web site index is not as much work as creating a sample book index, because a Web site usually contains less information than a book. The site should be large enough, with sufficient content, to support a good index. For example, I started out by creating an index of a 28-page site (with 24 of the pages indexable) resulting in 194 index entries. A second index was of a 45-page site (with 41 pages indexable) resulting in 161 index entries. Each of these projects took little time, and I then had useful sample indexes.

Your sample will need to be live and part of the Web site indexed, not merely a sample on your own Web site. A good way to find a site for your first sample index is to offer to create a free index to the owner of a Web site of an organization with which you have some affiliation. This could be your local public library, school, church, other community organization, municipality (if it is not too big), or a membership association to which you belong. Web sites of such organizations would most likely welcome volunteer contributions. You can also get your name and service known among the Web site's visitors, by insisting that your name and a link back to your own Web site appear at the bottom of the index page. This acknowledgment ought to be granted in exchange for a free service. For this reason you might consider choosing a site for a sample index that has many users or whose users might provide good contacts for future work referrals.

It's up to you if and for how long you also want to help maintain the free index. It's possible that the Web site owner will take it on. I found this to be the case for the index I created for a public library Web site, since librarians often have an interest in indexing.

2. Create or Update Your Own Web Site

Of course, it's very useful to have your own Web site if you are offering freelance services. If those services are Web-related, then you really must have your own Web site to confer some legitimacy on your claim of knowing how to work with Web sites.

Whether you have a Web site already or are still working on one, you should add a page for the services of Web site indexing. Having an entire Web page devoted to your Web site indexing services gives it more prominence. Labeling the page appropriately means it might even get picked up in search engine queries. For the content of the page, consider including the following:

- A short explanation of what a Web site index is (since it may not be obvious to all) and what its advantages are over other search methods
- A brief description of the procedure of Web site indexing and what tool you use
- Links to Web site indexes you have created
- Links to articles on Web site indexing and at least to the resource-rich Web Indexing SIG (www.web-indexing.org), regardless of whether you are a SIG member or not
- General information on rates, not an exact rate but perhaps a broad range, what you need to provide an estimate, or merely how you charge (hourly, per page, per index record, etc.). Also include information on project turnaround times.

Remember, for Web site indexing in particular, your Web site is not just to sell your services, but also to help inform and educate potential clients about Web site indexing in general. I do not recommend creating an index on your own site, however, unless the site is large enough. Otherwise, the small index looks kind of silly and does not provide a reasonable example of your work.

3. Offer Broader Web-Related Services

Since Web site indexing is a rather narrow service, you can increase your chance of getting contract work from Web site design firms or site owners by offering Web indexing as one of several services. Even though you may not be asked to create an index in your first job, doing related work helps to establish a relationship with the client. It might take time to raise client awareness of a need for an index. Alternatively, you might end up doing a larger package of services including indexing. Related services include creating the site map, creating a taxonomy, adding keywords for each page for search engine optimization, writing or editing Web content, and finally consulting or training in Web site index creation or in related areas of information architecture or content management.

Compared to an index, site maps are pretty straightforward to create. Clients could probably do this themselves, but might not have the time to devote to it. Ask the client to provide you with a diagram of the site's structure if at all possible. If not, you will have to rely on looking at the file structure through Windows Explorer. The HTML editing program Dreamweaver can also create a graphical site map for you to follow as you create the hyperlinked site map. You can create the site map by hand in your HTML editor, if the site is not too large, such as under 100 pages. If it is larger, you probably want to use a tool to extract the page titles with their URLs. Actually, you can use XrefHT for this task. Extract titles only and do no editing (make no subentries). Make the index. Then in your HTML editor, edit out all the letter headings and rearrange the title entries in the order that corresponds to the site structure. Consider putting the site map into columns (by creating a table).

An organization might prefer to create an index itself but would contract an indexer-consultant to train its in-house indexer on how to create the index or to edit and provide feedback for an index that it already created. The organization may find it more practical to create the index by someone on staff, if the Web site or intranet is still being created or growing simultaneously, and the indexing work is dragging out over time. A freelance Web site indexer, therefore, should position oneself as not merely an indexer but also a consultant/trainer.

4. Let Your Current Clients Know of Your New Service

Although it may seem that your current clients don't need Web site indexing services, they actually represent your best prospects. They know you, and you are familiar with their products. Explain to your indexing clients that you now also offer "HTML indexing for online content" and how this fits into their business. Even if they don't respond initially, they may come back to you in the future to request this type of work when they have a need for it.

Educational, professional, and textbook publishers, in particular, are branching into online media for their book content. If you have any periodical clients, they are also likely to be interested in Web-based indexes. Clients for whom you have indexed their catalogs (like a publisher's catalog of books) make especially good prospects, since you have already worked with them in a marketing mode. Finally, all organizations have Web sites, so you might also get to write the index for the publisher's own site.

5. Contact Organizations and Companies of Which You Are a Member or Client

While you will probably not have any luck cold calling the owners of Web sites, if you are a customer of the company or a member of the organization, they might pay more attention to you. In addition to community membership organizations, you might also consider your medical clinic, HMO, various insurance providers, banks, fitness or sports clubs, internet service providers, Web hosting services, utility companies, and so forth. To make the contact, don't just send an e-mail, but also follow up with a call or letter.

6. Network Locally

Even though the Web site indexing market has no geographic boundaries, networking with people you know is always more effective than networking with strangers. There are so many Web sites and intranets out there that could have indexes, and some are surely managed by people you may already know or could get to know face-to-face through local professional, networking, or community groups. If you find such local groups of Web designers or developers, usability experts, or information architects, you should attend their meetings. You can start by looking up the local chapters of national organizations.

7. Network Through the Larger Web Community

Make contact through e-mail and discussion groups with the types of people who are potential clients and not just the firms. In addition to providing job leads, these people can provide valuable information in helping you focus your marketing objectives. Sometimes you can get a very helpful e-mail from a stranger across the country. These people include:

- **Information architects** – Those responsible for the structural and organizational design of a site
- **Usability experts** – Those who work on making a site or software easier to use, including usability engineers, user experience engineers, and user testing specialists
- **Web designers** – Those who create Web sites in their entirety, or with an emphasis on the overall look and graphic design

- **Web developers** – Those who create Web sites, with an emphasis on the technology scripting to create interactive sites (forms, databases, animation, e-commerce, etc.)
- **Content management professionals** – Various professionals who consult on the implementation of content management systems

More information on such groups and discussion lists is listed at the end of this chapter.

8. Contact Web Design Firms

Other than the Web sites for which you already have some connections or specific interest, it doesn't make sense to contact Web sites one by one, for they cannot offer repeat work beyond index maintenance. As an analogy, rather than contacting authors one-by-one for book indexing, you contact publishers and packagers. So, for general marketing purposes, you should contact Web design firms, which have multiple Web site owner clients. "Web design" in this context is not limited to graphic design but includes full-service Web site creation. Thousands of such Web design companies have emerged in recent years, but many are simply independent individuals. It can be difficult to determine which ones among them are the larger firms, worthy for you to target. Although location does not matter, due to the large number of firms, you may as well start looking among local companies. Sometimes an initial onsite visit helps your prospects.

If you search the Web for directories of Web design firms, you will find numerous directory sites. But many of these are commercial directories that simply list anyone who pays them, including numerous small sole proprietorships. I recommend a more comprehensive search by one of the following means:

- Search the dmoz directory for full-service Web design firms and narrow the search by typing in your state or province in the search field (dmoz.org/Computers/Internet/Web_Design_and_Development/Designers/Full_Service/)
- Search in Google or another Web search engine on "largest Web design" + "your city name"
- The Firm List: Global Guide to Web Design/Development Firms (us.firmlist.com) is also quite comprehensive

The business research firm Forrester named the 17 largest Web design and development firms in the United States in July 2004 as (in alphabetical order): AGENCY.COM, AKQA, connect@jwt, Critical Mass, Digitas, Euro RSCG 4D, Grey Interactive, iDeutsch, IBM Global Services, Modern Media, Molecular, Organic, R/GA, Sapient, SBI.Razorfish, VML, and Zentropy Partners.

INDEXING RATES

Clients of freelance Web site indexing services tend to pay hourly, but they may also want an estimated total project cost or a maximum cost. The hourly rate you charge for Web site indexing should probably be a little more than the hourly rate you would charge for book indexing. According to the American Society of Indexers salary survey, the average hourly rate charged by freelance indexers, when they bill by the hour, in 2004 was $30–$34/hour, but when indexers charge by the page, the rate tends to come out higher. Although you might think you can charge significantly more for the specialized Web indexing skills, you may find out that the demand is not yet there for Web site indexing. If your fee goes too high, the potential client will decide the indexing project is not worth doing at all.

Estimating a project cost presents a challenge, especially for the first few projects. Unlike the printed page, Web pages within a Web site can vary greatly in length and quantity of indexable content. Nevertheless, you can still come up with a very rough estimate based on a total Web page count and per page rate. According to the American Society of Indexers Salary survey, the average rate charged by indexers in 2004 per indexable page was $3.26–$3.50, but the range varies depending upon the nature of the material. By skimming through several Web pages, going deeper down within the hierarchy of the site, you can get an idea if the pages have a lot of indexable content (i.e., long with several heading sections), or not so much, and you can determine your page rate for the total project estimate this way. Some pages are not suitable for indexing, namely intermediate directory pages lacking significant content other than a list of other pages in that section of the Web site. To be on the safe side, don't eliminate these from your page count.

You will have the extra task of inserting anchors, though. Therefore, you can let your client know that if the site does not already have anchors and headings so you have to insert them, this will add billable time to the project.

A rate per index entry is probably the fairest, but a majority of clients are not prepared to pay in this open-ended way. If the client is receptive to the idea, though, what you need to do is show your sample index and explain what it cost on the per-entry rate. This way the per-entry rate roughly translates into a per-project rate. To compare again with the book indexing rate, according to the American Society of Indexers Salary survey, the rate charged by indexers in 2004 per entry was $0.70–$0.79, but again the range varies greatly with the nature of the material.

INDEX MAINTENANCE

A question that needs to be answered, if possible, at the start of an indexing project is who will handle ongoing maintenance of the index as changes are made to the Web site. If you, the indexer, have the responsibility for maintaining the Web site or intranet, then without question it is your responsibility to keep the Web site index up to date. But if you are a freelance indexer for the project, either you can be retained for future updates, or you can provide guidelines and/or training to the Webmaster on how to maintain the index.

If you will maintain the index on a freelance basis for someone else's site, you also need to agree on:

- A schedule for updates: monthly or quarterly, for example, or on an ad hoc basis. If it is to be on an ad hoc basis, then you need to gain a relatively longer turn-around time for each assignment of such unscheduled work. For example, you cannot be expected to complete even a simple two-hour update job within only one day of being notified.
- The receipt of a list of file names that have been added or revised sufficiently to need new indexing. This way, you don't have to waste time searching for what has been changed.
- The form of delivery for index updates: a completely regenerated HTML index, an edited index HTML file, or strings of HTML code for the Webmaster to insert in the index. (Note that a regenerated HTML index works well only if there is not a lot of post-generated format editing of the index entries.)
- Whether you should also update the site map or any other directory on the Web site.
- A payment rate for updating, which would most likely be hourly with a one- or two-hour minimum.

If you are not being asked to update the index in the future, then you should provide written guidelines to the Webmaster on how to maintain the index. If applied, these guidelines will help ensure that your index continues to look good. If you link to the index as a sample of your work, a prospective client checking the index might deliberately test for the presence of new content in the index. In addition, you might also be able to add a little to your total project fee for this additional "consulting" service of writing index updating guidelines.

As for how to write the index maintenance guidelines, first determine what kinds of additions or changes to the Web site will most likely occur and which of these will affect the index. For example, the future content might include the occasional addition of summaries of future conferences. So, you would let the Webmaster know that conference summary pages should be indexed with: (1) the names of the speakers with a subentry for "conference presentation, [date]", (2) an entry for the main topic for each presentation with the subentry "conference presentation, [date]", and (3) the entry "conference presentation summaries" with the subentry for the date. Someone not even trained in indexing can follow the examples in the existing index and use your guidelines to keep the index at least satisfactorily updated. But you should encourage your client to come back to you with specific questions. If the questions are simple, you can answer for gratis, for you would want to stay on good terms with the client for potential referrals. If the questions are more involved, you can provide a simple partial answer and offer to go into more detail as a small paid consulting project.

CONCLUSION

While the potential need and demand for Web site indexes is great, the opportunities for freelancers to do this work are still in question. That does not mean, however, that there is not a role for freelancers. Instead of merely creating Web site indexes, freelance indexers can also offer consulting and training services or Web site index editing services. Discussion lists, such as the ones listed in the next section, can also be used for networking and marketing any of these services.

DISCUSSION LISTS AND OTHER RESOURCES FOR MARKETING

A good way to indirectly market is through posting on the mailing lists used by potential clients. Listed here are various professional communities, their professional associations, and some of their discussion lists.

Web Design

WebDesign-L, www.webdesign-l.com

Originally created in early 1997 to address both "page design" and "site architecture." It has a rather high volume of messages, some of which are technical with respect to Web development.

Highfivebabble, groups.yahoo.com/group/highfivebabble, or Babblelist, www.babblelist.com

Despite the two URLS and two names, this is one group, established in 2000, with over 1,365 members.

"thelist", lists.evolt.org/mailman/listinfo/thelist

A discussion list for designers, developers, and Web managers. It's affiliated with the evolt.org Web site, an advertising-supported collection of articles and resources.

Sitepoint forums, www.sitepoint.com/forums

A collection of numerous specialized forums on Web site design, programming, and marketing.

Information Architecture (IA)

Information Architecture Institute, iainstitute.org

This is the main international professional association of information architects.

SIGIA-L, mail.asis.org/mailman/listinfo/sigia-l
This is the discussion list affiliated with the Information Architecture SIG of the American Society for Information Science and Technology (ASIST). You don't have to be a member of the SIG to join the list.

Usability and Computer–Human Interaction (CHI or HCI)

ACM SIGCHI, www.acm.org/sigchi
This is the Special Interest Group on Computer–Human Interaction of ACM (the Association for Computing Machinery).

SIGHCI-L, mail.asis.org/mailman/listinfo/sighci-l
This is the discussion list affiliated with the Human–Computer Interaction SIG of the American Society for Information Science and Technology (ASIST). You don't have to be a member of the SIG to join the list.

Content Management (CM)

CM Professionals, www.cmprofessionals.org
This is a relatively new professional association for what is hoped to be a new field of consultants to work with content management systems.

CMS Lists, www.cms-lists.org
This site offers a directory of content management lists, some restricted to CM Professionals members and some not.

Taxonomies

Taxonomy Community of Practice, finance.groups.yahoo.com/group/TaxoCoP
Started only in 2005, this public Yahoo! group has become very active.

Taxonomy Community of Practice wiki, taxocop.wikispaces.com
This is not so much a forum as a resource of information on the growing field of taxonomies.

Intranets

There isn't a single professional association dedicated to people who work with intranets, but there are several Web sites with good resources on the subject. They tend to be advertising-supported collections of articles, tips, and links.

Intranet Journal, www.intranetjournal.com
Intranet Journal discussion group, forums.datamation.com/forumdisplay.php?s=&forumid=8
CIO online magazine section on intranets, www.cio.com/km/intranet/index.html
Complete Intranet Resource, www.intrack.com/intranet

Intranet 101.com, www.intranet101.com
Intranet Roadmap, www.intranetroadmap.com/default.cfm

FURTHER READING

"ASI Salary Survey 2004." *Key Words*. Vol. 13, No. 1. January–March 2005, pp. 16–21.

Barnum, Carol et al. "Index Versus Full-Text Search: A Usability Study of User Preference and Performance." *Technical Communication*. Vol. 51, No. 2. May 2004, pp. 185–206.

Leise, Fred. "Metadata and Content Management Systems: An Introduction for Indexers." *The Indexer*. Vol. 24. No. 2. October 2004, p. 71.

Morris, Jeff. "Putting It Together: Taxonomy, Classification & Search." *Intelligent Enterprise*. September 2003. www.transformmag.com/db_area/archs/2003/09/tfm0309f2_1.shtml

Morville, Peter. *Ambient Findability*. Sebastopol, CA: O'Reilly Media, Inc., 2005.

Morville, Peter and Louis Rosenfeld. *Information Architecture for the World Wide Web: Designing Large-Scale Web Sites*, 2nd edition. Sebastopol, CA: O'Reilly Media, Inc., 2002.

Spool, Jared M. "Why On-Site Searching Stinks." User Interface Engineering. September 1, 1997. www.uie.com/articles/search_stinks

About the Author

Heather Hedden has been providing services and training in indexing (Web sites, books, and periodicals), taxonomy creation, and Web site design through her business Hedden Information Management since 2004. Prior to that, she served more than 10 years as an in-house periodical indexer and then senior vocabulary editor at the Gale Group. In early 2007, she joined the Viziant Corporation as its information taxonomist. After leaving Gale, she learned back-of-the-book indexing from Seth Maislin's Middlesex Community College class and Web site indexing from Kevin Broccoli's online course. Since 2005, Heather has been teaching her own online courses in Web site indexing, both independently and through the Continuing Education Program of Simmons College Graduate School of Library and Information Science.

Heather has also given various conference presentations and workshops on Web site indexing and has published numerous articles on the subject, appearing in *Computers in Libraries*, *Intranets*, *The Indexer*, *Key Words*, and other publications. Heather reactivated the Web Indexing Special Interest Group (SIG) of the American Society of Indexers and was the SIG's coordinator in 2005 and 2006. Also in 2006, Heather was president of the New England Chapter of the American Society of Indexers. In addition to her membership in the American Society of Indexers (ASI), Heather is also a member of the Information Architecture Institute. Heather has a BA from Cornell University and an MA from Princeton University.

Index

Linda Kenny Sloan

Figures and tables are denoted by "f" and "t" following page numbers.

A

Alphabetical sorting. *See* Sorting
American Society of Indexers (ASI)
    Web Indexing SIG, 10
Anchors, 101–102
    finding and creating, 101
    in HTML Indexer, 80, 89
    in XRefHT, 64–66, 67–69
Audience awareness, 100
    focus on specific interest, 106
Australian Society of Indexers' Web Indexing Prize, 9
A-Z indexes. *See* Web site indexes
A-Z ribbon of navigation letters. *See* Navigation letters

B

Book indexes. *See* Online book indexes
Book indexing software
    CINDEX, 45–49. *See also* CINDEX
    hyperlinking coding into index entries, 43–44
    Macrex, 51–52
    SKY Index Professional, 49–51. *See also* SKY Index Professional
Books on Web site indexing, 11
Brenner, Diane, ix, 10
Broccoli, Kevin, ix, 10
Brown, David M., 9, 38, 79
Browne, Glenda, 10
Browser (Web) use
    anchor identification, 101
    bottom of page display, 106
    external URL indexing, 92
    file names, obtaining, 35
    HTML Indexer and, 84–85
    indexing process, 70, 90
    XRefHT and, 127
Bulleted lists, 20, 32–33, 36, 75, 130–132
Business and index market. *See also* Marketing services
    index maintenance agreement, 149–151
    indexing rates, 148
    market overview, 137–140
    site types suitable for indexing, 135–137

C

Capitalization of main entries, 129
Cascading style sheets (CSS), 33–34, 46, 95–96, 133. *See also* Style sheets
Changeability of Web sites, 136
CINDEX
    cascading style sheets in, 46

CINDEX (*cont.*)
  index conversion in XRefHT, 56
  index editing in, 48–49
  index preparation for HTML/Prep, 54
  markup tags, 47–48
  page range default change to hyphen, 46
  saving as HTML tagged text, 45–46
Client relationships, 146–147, 149–151
Columns in index, 128–129
Content management resources, 152
Converting indexes into HTML
  book indexing software-created indexes, 44, 45, 49
  HTML/Prep for, 52–56
  printed indexes for dual outputs, 58–59
  software utilities for, 9, 38
  XRefHT for, 56–58
Courses in Web site indexing, viii
Craven, Timothy, ix, 38, 61–62, 75
Cross-references, 4–5
  creating, 110–115, 113*t*
  editing and creating in XRefHT, 71–73
  editing in HTML Indexer, 91–92
  in HTML Indexer, 90–93, 91*f*
  internal links, 23, 30
  see also references, 112–114
  see references, 4–5, 111–112, 113*t*
  style options for, 114–115
CSS. *See* Cascading style sheets

D

Databases for indexes, 125, 126*f*, 139
Dedicated back-of-the-book indexing software. *See* Book indexing software
Dedicated web site indexing software. *See* Book indexing software
Definition lists, 20–21, 31–32, 36, 130–131

Discussion lists, 151–152

E

Editing indexes, 125–127
  in CINDEX, 48–49
  in HTML Indexer, 88–90
  in SKY Index Professional, 51
  in XRefHT, 69–73
Entries. *See* Index entries

F

Faceted search, 143–144
FAR HTML online help software, 39–41
Fees for indexing, 149
File transfer protocol (FTP), 27–28
Font, 16, 30
Formatting
  A-Z navigation bar hyperlinks to letter sections, 128
  columns, 128–129
  indenting entries, 31–34, 36
  subentries, 130–133
  lists, 32–33
  lower/upper case for index entries, 129–130
  non breaking spaces (HTML), 32
  sort options (HTML Indexer), 90
  text formatting tags, 14–15, 16
  top of page links, 129
Frames
  as enhanced content to index page, 95
  index in, 39–40, 88
  index navigation letters in, 7*f*, 93, 128
  as pages to index, 104*f*
  for periodical index citation lists, 125
Freelance services, Web sites for, 145–146

FTP (File transfer protocol), 27–28
Function pages, 103–104

G

Graphics, 17–18, 108, 130
Groups, online, 151–152

H

Headings, index. *See* Index entries
Headings, Web page
   choosing for indexing, 67–68, 105–107
   imprecise and vague section, 108–109
   links to, 93–94
   main and subentries, 86–88
Hedden, Heather, 9–10
Help files and online help, 38–41
   index types in HTML Indexer, 95
Henninger, Maureen, 9
Home page, 102
HTML anchors. *See* Anchors
HTML editing software
   listing of, 25–27
   Web index completion with, 34–36
HTML external URLs
   in HTML Indexer, 90–91
   links to, 24–25
HTML Indexer, 9
   adding anchors, 89
   adding files and entries, 85–88, 86*f*, 88*f*
   cross-references, 90–93, 91*f*
   HTML anchors, 80
   index files
      editing, 88–90
      generating, 90
      saving, 84
   index style and settings in, 93–96, 94*f*
   main and subentries, 86–88
   modifications of indexed files, 96
   non-HTML pages, 81–82

   panes
      index entry, 83–84
      project tree, 82–83
   sort options, 88, 89–90
   URL adding and editing, 80–81, 90–91
      external URLs, 92–93
   viewing files, 84–85
HTML pages
   editing anchors and pages, 63–69, 125–127
   head content tags for, 18–19
   uploading, 27–28
   viewing code, 25
HTML tags
   break tag, 15
   images, 17–18
   link tags, 21–25
   list tags, 19–21
   metadata, 19
   page head content tags, 15–16, 18–19
   table creation, 17
   text formatting tags, 14–15, 16
HTML/Prep, 9
   index conversion features, 52–53
   index preparation for, 53–54
   running program, 54–56, 55*f*
Hypertext links
   A-Z indexes and, 29–31
   handling multiple locators in hypertext, 123
   instead of page numbers, 3–4
   making page links, 36

I

Images, 17–18, 108
Indenting subentries, 31–34, 36, 130–131
Index conversion software, 9, 38, 52–59
   conversion of printed indexes to HTML, 58–59

Index conversion software (*cont.*)
  HTML/Prep, 52–56
  XRefHT as, 58–59
Index entries
  clarity and context of, 119
  conciseness of, 118
  HTML Indexer, creating in, 86–88
  keyword placement, 118–119
  length of, 117–118
  multiple locators in hypertext, 123
  periodical Web indexes, 124–125, 126*f*
  subentries. *See* Subentries
  sub-subentries (third level). *See* Sub-subentries
  term grammar, 119–120
Index files
  generating from HTML Indexer, 90
  generating from SKY Index Professional, 50–51
  generating from XRefHT, 75–76
  layout, 94–95
Index structure, 3–5. *See also* Index entries
  subentries and, 120–121
Index style
  back-of-the-book, 6, 58
  bulleted entries, 132–133
  case of entries, 129
  columns, 128–129
  cross-references, 72, 111, 114–115
  font, 130
  formatting options, 127–128, 134
  HTML coding for, 16
  HTML Indexer options for, 93–96
  line spacing, 132
  main entries, 117–120
  navigation letters, 5, 93–94, 128
  online help, 39–40
  subentries, 120–125
  XRefHT options for, 75–76
Indexing process
  creating subentries, 120–125
  named entities, 109–110
  wording of entries, 117–120
  in XRefHT, 70, 73–76
Indexing Research. *See* CINDEX
INDTOHTM index conversion software, 9
Information architecture, 1–2
Intranet indexing
  market for, 139–140
  online help files and, 39
  resources, 152–153
  types of, 5–6
  user input to, 110

J

Jermey, Jonathan, 9, 10

K

Keyword index, generated from XRefHT, 76

L

Lamb, James, ix, 10
Letter bar for A-Z indexes. *See* Navigation letters
Leverage Technologies, 9. *See also* Ream, David
Line spacing, 132
Link tags
  internal links, 22
  page links, 23–24, 29–30
  Web site to web site (external links), 24–25
Lists
  definition lists, 20–21, 31–32, 36, 130–131
  ordered lists, 20
  subentry indenting with, 32–33
  tags for, 19–21
  unordered (bulleted) lists, 20, 32–33, 36, 75, 130–132
Locators, 3–4
  in CINDEX, 45–46, 48–49

converting from print, 58
converting with HTML/Prep, 53
converting with XRefHT, 56
hyperlinking, 36, 43–44, 48–49, 51
in Macrex, 51
multiple for same entry, 3, 122
at named anchors, 64, 67, 101
in SKY Index, 49–51

M

Macintosh system, 61
Macrex
 hypertext markup menu and definition files, 51–52
Maintenance of Web site index, 96, 130, 149–151
Maislin, Seth, vi, ix
Mapper, 44, 45, 59
Marketing services, 144–148
 mix of services, 146
 networking and, 146–148
 resources, 151–153
 Web design firms, 148
 Web site and index for, 144–146
Markup tags, 47–48
Meisheid, Bill, 10
Menus, navigation, 103, 141
Metadata, 140
 HTML tags, 19
 keyword index, 76

N

Named anchors. *See* Anchors
Names, indexing of, 109–110
Navigation letters, 5
 CINDEX indexes and, 48, 49
 creating in HTML editor, 37
 formatting options, 128
 in frames, 7*f*
 HTML Indexer settings for, 93–94
 HTML/Prep feature, 53
 hyperlinking of, 23, 30–31

Macrex indexes and, 52
SKY indexes and, 51
Navigation pages, Web site, 103

O

Online book indexes, 6*f*
 converting printed indexes to HTML, 58–59
 market for, 137–138
Online help files, 39
Online help indexing, 38–41
 index types in HTML Indexer, 95
Online resources, 151–152
Ordered lists, 20

P

Page indexing, order of, 100
Page locators. *See* Locators
Pages, Web. *See* Web pages
PDF indexing, 81, 93, 104–105, 130, 139
Periodical indexes, 8*f*
 index entries in, 124–125, 126*f*
 market for, 139
 multiple dates following entry, 125*f*
Printed index to HTML conversion, 58–59

R

Ream, David, viii, 60
Revising Web site indexes, 96, 130, 149–151
Rhoades, Gale, viii, 51, 60
RoboHelp online help software, 39
Rowland, Marilyn, ix

S

Sample Web index preparation, 144–145
Schreiner, Kamm, viii

Scrollable frame indexes, 39–40
Search engines, 140–141
Search methods
    faceted search, 143–144
    metadata, 19, 76, 140
    navigation menus, 103, 141
    search engines, 19, 140–141
    site maps, 141–143, 142f, 146
    taxonomies, 143
"See" and "see also" references. *See* Cross-references
Selecting page sections (headings) to index, 105–107
Selecting Web pages to index, 102–105
Site maps, 102, 141–143, 142f, 146
Size of Web site, considerations, 135–136
SKY Index Professional
    editing Web page index in, 51
    index preparation for HTML/Prep, 54
    URL entry into, 49–50
Software
    book indexing. *See* Book indexing software
    conversion. *See* Index conversion software
    HTML editing. *See* HTML editing software
    Web indexing. *See* Web indexing software
Sorting
    HTML editors and, 34
    by HTML Indexer, 88, 89–90
    hyperlinks and, 44
    indexing software feature, 34
    by XRefHT, 73–74
Spaces, non-breaking, 32
Special Interest Group (SIG), Web Indexing (ASI), 10
Spell-checking, 74, 77, 97
Style, index. *See* Index style

Style sheets. *See also* Cascading style sheets (CSS)
    CINDEX HTML-tagged text and, 46
    CINDEX-generated HTML/Prep-tagged text and, 54
    HTML Indexer and, 95–96
    indenting subentries, 33–34, 130–132
    underlining in hypertext, removing by, 22
    usage, 133
    XRefHT for converting indexes and, 57
Subentries
    converting with HTML/Prep, 53
    converting with XRefHT, 56–58
    cross-references and, 4–5, 30, 71–72, 91, 111–113
    editing, 12
    HTML editor use on, 34, 36
    HTML Indexer and, 86–87
    hyperlinking, 3–4, 43–44
    indenting in HTML, 31–34, 36, 130–131
    line spacing, 132
    run-in, 75
    techniques for creating, 120–125
    XRefHT and, 62, 70–71
Sub-subentries
    creation of, 47, 57, 62, 71, 87
    usage, 121–122

T

Table creation tags, 17
Tags. *See* HTML tags
Taxonomies, 143, 152
Text formatting tags, 14–15, 16
Third-level entries. *See* Sub-subentries
Tools
    index conversion. *See* Index conversion software
    Web indexing. *See* Web indexing software

Topic choice, 107–110
Top-of-page links, 129
Training services, 146

U

Universal resource locators. *See* URLs
Unordered lists, 20, 32–33, 36, 75, 130–132
Unwalla, Mike, 87, 92
Updating Web site indexes, 96, 130, 149–151
Uploading Web pages, 27–28
URLs
    adding and editing in HTML Indexer, 80–81
    cross-reference links in HTML Indexer, 92–93
    external URLs in HTML Indexer, 90–91
    index conversion preparation, 56
    inserting in book indexing software, 43–44
Usability resources, 152
User focus, 100
Utilities, index conversion
    HTML/Prep, 52–56. *See also* HTML/Prep
    XRefHT, 56–58. *See also* XRefHT

V

Van Ravensway, Gerry, 10
Viewing
    HTML source code, 25
    Web pages to be indexed in browser, 35, 70, 84–85, 90, 101
VisualSpeller, 74, 77

W

Walker, Dwight, ix, 9, 38
Web browser use. *See* Browser (Web) use

Web design resources, 151–152
Web Indexing Prize of Australian Society of Indexers, 9
Web Indexing SIG (ASI), 10
Web indexing software, 37–41. *See also* Index conversion software
    dedicated standalone Web indexing, 38
    HTML Indexer. *See* HTML Indexer
    HTML/Prep, 9, 52–56
    indenting formats supported, 130–132, 131*f*
    index conversion utilities, 9, 38
    online help authoring software, 38–41
    XRefHT. *See* XRefHT
Web pages
    choosing pages to index, 102–105
    copying page file names, 35
    data extraction with XRefHT, 62–67, 63*f*
    database query link to intermediate page, 125*f*
    dynamically generated, 104*f*
    functions on, 103–104, 103*f*
    home page, 102
    indexing order for, 100–101
    non-HTML pages, 81–82, 104–105
    uploading and viewing, 27–28, 101
Web site indexes
    content review, 110
    defined, 2–3
    hypertext links in, 29–31
    indexing entire site, 7*f*
    information architecture and, 1–2
    intranets, 5–6, 139–140, 152–153
    maintenance and modifications to, 93–96, 149–151
    market overview, 137–140
    navigation letters in, 5, 30–31, 37, 128
    online book indexes, 6*f*, 137–138
    periodical indexes, 8*f*, 139

Web site indexes (cont.)
    sample indexes for marketing, 144–145
    site types suitable for indexing, 6–8, 135–137
    structure of, 3–5
    types of, 5–8
Web site indexing
    approach to, 99–102
    A-Z navigation bar, 5
    books on, 11
    choosing topics to index, 108
    frames and generated pages, 104f
    history of, 9–10
    software for, 37–41
Webb, Kerry, 9
WEBIX index conversion software, 9
Weblinkr index conversion software, 9
wINDEX, 52, 59
Word processor use, 34–35, 36–37

Wright, Jan C., 10

X

XRefHT, 9, 61–62
    anchors
        adding, 67–69
        editing and extracting, 64–66
    autoanchor option in file menu, 68–69
    converting indexes, 56–58, 57f
    cross-references, 71–73
    extracting Web page data, 62–67, 63f, 65f
    generating index, 75–76
    index editing, 69–74, 71f, 73f
    indexing process and tools, 70
    keyword index, 76
    sorting the index, 73–74
    spell check, 74
    sub-subentries, 71

More Great Books for Indexing Professionals

Indexing Specialties: Scholarly Books
Edited by Margie Towery and Enid L. Zafran

This skillfully edited book covers the indexing of scholarly books in a number of key fields, including economics, public policy, philosophy, law, and music. The topic of foreign languages in scholarly indexing is given close attention, and John Bealle's account of his experiences in indexing his own work will be welcomed by academic author-indexers. Tying the book together is Margie Towery's essay on what constitutes quality in scholarly indexing.

Softbound • ISBN 978-1-57387-236-2

ASI Members $28.00 • Nonmembers $35.00

Genealogy and Indexing
Edited by Kathleen Spaltro

Indexes are the essential search tool for genealogists, and this timely book fills a conspicuous void in the literature. Kathleen Spaltro and contributors take an in-depth look at the relationship between indexing and genealogy and explain how genealogical indexes are constructed. They offer practical advice to indexers who work with genealogical documents as well as genealogists who want to create their own indexes. Noeline Bridge's chapter on names will quickly become the definitive reference for trying to resolve questions on variants, surname changes, and foreign designations. Other chapters discuss software, form and entry, the need for standards, and the development of after-market indexes.

Softbound • ISBN 978-1-57387-163-1

ASI Members $25.00 • Nonmembers $31.25

Software for Indexing
Edited by Sandi Schroeder

In this thorough review of the software products used in indexing, professional indexers share their favorite features, tips, and techniques. Starting with a chapter on dedicated indexing programs, CINDEX, MACREX, SKY Index, and wINDEX are compared. Coverage of embedding software includes Framemaker, Microsoft Word, PageMaker, QuarkXPress, Ixgen, Index Tool Professional, and IndeXTension. For those interested in online and Web indexing, HTML/Prep, HTML Indexer, and RoboHelp are all covered. Other chapters discuss database software, customized software that works with dedicated programs, and automatic and machine-aided indexing.

Softbound • ISBN 978-1-57387-166-2

ASI Members $28.00 • Nonmembers $35.00

Index It Right! Advice from the Experts, Volume 1
Edited by Enid L. Zafran

Here is the premiere title in a new series presenting selected expert coverage in key indexing areas. Volume 1 includes top tips and advice on indexing philosophy (Carol Roberts), theology (Kate Mertes), biography (Martin L. White), horticulture (Thérèse Shere with Lina B. Burton), art (Susan DeRenne Coerr), encyclopedias (Merion Lerner-Levine), computer manuals (Beth Palmer), and Web sites (Fred Brown).

Softbound • ISBN 978-1-57387-237-9

ASI Members $28.00 • Nonmembers $35.00

Indexing Specialties: History
Edited by Margie Towery

This compilation of articles focuses on the indexing of history textbooks, art history, medieval and Renaissance history, Latin American history, and gender and sexual orientation language issues. The authors' intelligent advice and discussions will assist both new and experienced indexers who work in the field of history and related disciplines.

Softbound • ISBN 978-1-57387-055-9

ASI Members $12.00 • Nonmembers $18.00

Indexing Specialties: Psychology
Edited by Becky Hornyak

Continuing the series that addresses specialized areas for indexers, Becky Hornyak has assembled a panel of experts that includes Sandy Topping, Carolyn Weaver, and Carol Schoun. The emphasis is on indexing textbooks and books aimed at clinical practitioners in the field of psychology. Includes extensive, annotated listings of print and other resources for psychology indexers.

Softbound • ISBN 978-1-57387-149-5

ASI Members $20.00 • Nonmembers $25.00

To order directly from the publisher, include $4.95 postage and handling for the first book ordered and $1.00 for each additional book. Catalogs also available upon request.
Order online at www.infotoday.com and specify that you are an ASI member when ordering.

Information Today, Inc.

143 Old Marlton Pike, Medford, NJ 08055

(800)300-9868 (609)654-6266 custserv@infotoday.com